Too Deep for Words

Too Deep for Words

A Theology of Liturgical Expression

CLAYTON J. SCHMIT

Westminster John Knox Press
LOUISVILLE • LONDON

Scripture quotations, unless otherwise indicated, are from the New Revised Standard Version of the Bible, copyright © 1989 by the Division of Christian Education of the National Council of the Churches of Christ in the U.S.A., and used by permission.

Scripture quotations marked RSV are from the Revised Standard Version of the Bible, copyright © 1946, 1952, 1971, and 1973 by the Division of Christian Education of the National Council of the Churches of Christ in the U.S.A., and are used by permission.

Excerpt from *Are You the Friendly God* by Brian Wren, © 1989 Hope Publishing Company, Carol Stream, IL 60188. All rights reserved. Used by permission.

Excerpt from *Eternal Spirit of the Living Christ* by Frank von Christierson, © 1974 The Hymn Society (admin. Hope Publishing Company, Carol Stream, IL 60188). All rights reserved. Used by permission.

Excerpt from *God Is Here!* by Fred Pratt Green, © 1979 Hope Publishing Company, Carol Stream, IL 60188. All rights reserved. Used by permission.

Excerpt from "Processing," by Janet Schlichting, *Assembly* (December 1979). All rights reserved. Used by permission.

Book design by Sharon Adams
Cover design by Night & Day Design
Cover photograph of dancer © Stephen Wilkes/Allsport/Getty Images

First edition
Published by Westminster John Knox Press
Louisville, Kentucky

This book is printed on acid-free paper that meets the American National Standards Institute Z39.48 standard. ♾

PRINTED IN THE UNITED STATES OF AMERICA
02 03 04 05 06 07 08 09 10 11 — 10 9 8 7 6 5 4 3 2 1

Library of Congress Cataloging-in-Publication Data

Schmit, Clayton J.
    Too deep for words : a theology of liturgical expression / Clayton J. Schmit.—1st ed.
    p. cm.
    Includes bibliographical references and index.
    ISBN 0-664-22392-3 (alk. paper)
    1. Public worship. 2. Preaching. 3. Aesthetics—Religious aspects—Christianity. 4. Oral communication—Religious aspects—Christianity. I. Title.

BV15 .S335 2002
264—dc21

2001056770

For Carol Vallely Schmit

Contents

Preface

When people go to seminary to learn the skills of pastoral leadership, they usually entertain the presumption that they will learn to do certain things well. They will not merely learn the rudiments of preaching and leading worship, but they will learn techniques that will be useful to God's people and they will learn evaluative skills that can be used during their ministries as means to calculate their pastoral effectiveness. Along the way, much is learned that is, by and large, very useful in the practice of ministry. But among the things not learned—in most cases I dare say—is the means by which to determine how well one preaches or leads in worship. These are the activities that pastors and lay ministers perform each week. These are the most public elements of ministry. These are the pastoral skills that are most visible to the people who gather for a divine encounter each Sunday. Given so much practice and visibility, why is it that preaching in this country is facing such a crisis? Why do worshipers sense that pastors and worship leaders do not know the difference between doing the job and doing the job well? And, with all their training, why do seminary graduates arrive at the end of their formal theological education asking the kinds of questions that I asked upon my own seminary graduation: "What *is* a good sermon? What does it mean to prepare and lead worship effectively? How can I tell when I have done a decent job? Or an excellent one? Or a poor one?"

The fruits of this particular project are an attempt on my part to answer some of those questions. As a seminary teacher of preaching and worship myself, I now see that providing *basic* instruction in the skills of preaching and worship leadership are the main fruits of our work while students are with us. Those who wish to consider the next phase, what it means to be highly effective, are the ministers who proceed beyond the required fundamentals courses and beyond seminary graduation to be continuing students of theology and practice. It is hoped that the conversation undertaken here will prove useful for preachers and worship leaders who continue to struggle with how to perform their roles with excellence both for the sake of the faith and for the sake of God's people.

While it is impossible for me to determine the exact starting point of the dialogue that has led to this project, it is easy to pinpoint the opportunity and the conversation partners that have allowed for its emergence as a book. Although I wish to thank those responsible for enabling me to write it, I hold none of them responsible for any errors or inconsistencies in its pages. In large measure, the inspiration is theirs; yet the responsibility for the state of the dialogue as presented here is solely mine. With deep gratitude, I wish to thank: Duke Divinity School and the Henry Luce Foundation for the opportunity (The Luce Postdoctoral Fellowship in Preaching) that allowed me the time to reflect and write; Richard Lischer, William H. Willimon, and William C. Turner, Duke homiletics faculty who nurtured me as a person, preacher, and teacher; J. Bob Levison, Karen Westerfield Tucker, and Richard Hays, Duke faculty who offered friendship and conversation; James L. Crenshaw, who provided companionship and a pond on which to reflect; Elijah Keck, who provided his father's friendship and perspective; Charles L. Bartow of Princeton Theological Seminary, whose undying support and academic guidance have crafted a scholar out of a pastor; Pastors Diane Dardón, Timothy Kellgren, Robert Kaul, and Dennis Tollefson, partners in proclamation who read versions of this manuscript and provided practical advice from the perspective of the parish; and Thomas G. Long, formerly of Westminster John Knox and Geneva Press, for his guiding interest in bringing this project to publication. I thank also my parents, Gene and Marcie Schmit, for seeing to it that gathering for worship with God's people and attending to the Word became life habits that were to feed my faith and point me toward a profession. Similarly, I thank Kyrie and Jacob Schmit, who teach me the practical significance of these things through shared ritual and story. Finally, and most sincerely, I thank my attorney, who has for fourteen years kept me professionally out of hot water and personally in a warm and strong covenant of marriage, Carol L. Vallely.

Clayton J. Schmit
March 19, 2001, Third Monday in Lent
Fuller Theological Seminary
Pasadena, California

Introduction

The Spirit helps us in our weakness; for we do not know how to pray as we ought, but that very Spirit intercedes with sighs too deep for words.

Rom. 8:26

People who preach, pray, and lead in public worship are, whether they like to acknowledge it or not, performers. Their public use of speech, gesture, and movement is different from their private or intimate ways of communicating. Gestures are grander so that they can be seen by all in the worshiping assembly. Movement is planned and should be smooth and elegant, some would even say choreographed.[1] And speech is carefully crafted and delivered so as to draw the assembly into a unified activity and to touch them deeply. In other words, there is an artistic quality to all that worship leaders and preachers do.

Of central concern to those who engage in such artistic presentations is how to do them well. How can preachers craft their language in such a way as to give authentic and meaningful expression to the Word of God in the context of the congregation? How can the words of worship leaders draw people into the activity of worshiping together and make the presence of Christ known to them? How can the words of public prayer be crafted in such a way as to unite the assembly's hearts, draw worshipers into conversation with their Creator, and express the deeply felt needs, wants, and praise of the people?

How to do these things well is the topic of this book. It is intended to be used by those already engaged in the ministries of preaching and worship leadership, whether ordained or lay, and for those who are training to undertake such ministries. It is written from the perspective of one who is a Lutheran pastor and scholar. Additionally, as a pastoral musician I have had the opportunity to perform and lead in worship in a wide array of ecumenical settings in this and other countries. Thus, the ideas and reflections in this work not only are born of my experience as a North American Lutheran but also derive from the experience of worship in many other denominations and cultures. It is my hope, therefore, that the ideas presented here can be part of a conversation that takes place both within and outside my own community of faith. The intention is to discuss effective language use in preaching and leading public worship.

The arts involved in worship can be many: dance, drama, music, visual arts, sculpture, poetry, and so on. The particular focus of this investigation will be limited to those aspects of worship that have to do with preaching, public prayer, and the general language of worship leadership. The study will center principally on the theological and aesthetic issues that have to do with the use of verbal liturgical expression.

Expression has to do with making personal thoughts, feelings, or states of mind known to others. "An utterance," says Simon Blackburn in the *Oxford Dictionary of Philosophy*, "expresses a thought; a cry expresses grief or pain; a poem may express nostalgia or energy."[2] Expression is involved in all our speech and in every form of communication. It certainly is involved in how we convey messages and meaning in Christian worship. Those who speak in leadership roles in worship are engaged in the expression not only of their own thoughts but of the needs of the community of faith, the tenets of the faith, and the Word of God.

Expression also has to do with aesthetic theory. The philosophical view is that works of art derive their effect by expressing something that is interior to the artist. Such theories were developed by modern thinkers. In postmodern consideration, expression in art takes on a multivalent quality as art attempts to bring into juxtaposition elements of diverse styles that barrage the percipient with clashing and incongruous images. The purpose of such incongruity is to call into question any sense of objective meaning in art.[3] Part of the postmodern attitude, as Stanley J. Grenz defines it, is "a desire to challenge the power of modernity as invested in institutions and canonical traditions."[4] Yet, the arts found in Christian worship are designed not to undo the canons and institutions of the church, but to advance them. Thus, the original philosophical disposition regarding expression will inform us as we proceed.

The purpose here will be to consider the ways that verbal expression in worship is related to what we know about aesthetic expression and to show that there are theological connections between them. The theological considerations have to do with the understanding that at times, words fail us and that *mere* language cannot express fully what is in the hearts of believers who worship and pray. There are those times when in our weakness, we do not know how to pray as we ought and, as Paul assures us, "the Spirit intercedes for us with sighs too deep for words." But, as we will see, preachers and worship leaders can find ways to give expression to those thoughts and feelings that are "too deep for words." These ways of using words have to do with artistic expression, performance, and the poetic use of language. *The purpose of this book will be to demonstrate the aesthetic significance of verbal liturgical expression and the aesthetic responsibility of those who preach, pray, and lead in public worship.*

Along the way, several theological assertions will be made. The subtitle, "A Theology of Liturgical Expression," is offered for clarity, but it is not used to suggest that this project constitutes a fully developed theological system. The ideas contained here derive from Scripture and from consideration of liturgical, philosophical, and performance theory principles. They do represent a theological way of understanding the nature of liturgical expression. The hope is, however, that the thoughts expressed here are merely the beginning of a dialogue about the aesthetic implications of what we say and do in worship.

The book is organized in two parts. In chapters 1 through 4, philosophical and theoretical issues will provide the basis for deriving a theological stance with regard to liturgical expression. Chapter 1 examines the nature of art and demonstrates the need for artistic expression in preaching and worship leadership. The second chapter looks into the ways that God is present and active in worship and the roles of preachers and worship leaders as performers who have a responsibility to disclose the divine presence. Drawing on the philosophical work of J. L. Austin, the third chapter considers the performatory (or performative) power of liturgical language. The concluding chapter of part 1 draws together the philosophical and theological principles under consideration in a discussion of the need for preachers and the leaders of public prayer and worship to perform their roles with excellence.

Part 2 of the book turns to the practical matter of demonstrating how preachers and worship leaders can perform their roles with aesthetic sensitivity. Chapter 5 deals with the poetic dimensions of preaching and concludes with an examination of poetic tools and some examples and exercises to foster creative use of language. Chapter 6 has to do with the art of public prayer; it also provides examples and exercises to guide those who craft prayers for public worship. Chapter 7 considers the importance of aesthetic responsivity in relation to the use of the miscellaneous language of worship (for example, announcements and liturgical directions).

PART 1

1

Art for Faith's Sake

God is here! As we your people meet to offer praise and prayer,
May we find in fuller measure what it is in Christ we share.
Here, as in the world around us, all our varied skills and arts
Wait the coming of the Spirit into open minds and hearts.

Here are symbols to remind us of our life-long need of grace;
Here are table, font, and pulpit; here the cross has central place.
Here in honesty of preaching, here in silence, as in speech,
Here, in newness and renewal, God the Spirit comes to each.

"God Is Here," st. 1 and 2
Fred Pratt Green

Speechless. That was the state in which Zechariah was left when he was confronted by an angel and told that he and his barren wife Elizabeth would have a son (Luke 1:5–20). It was also, as Mark's Gospel tells us, the state of the women who discovered that Jesus was not in the tomb on Easter morning. They ran away in terror and "said nothing to anyone, for they were afraid" (Mark 16:8). An encounter with God can take your breath away—and your speech. And yet it is precisely through speech that we pass on the stories of divine encounter. Sooner or later, those who wish to give testimony to the ways that God has touched their lives will seek to express themselves using language. Zechariah's speech returned just in time to name the boy John. The voices of the women returned, at some point, to spread the news of Jesus' resurrection.

There are other modes of expression besides speech. But speech is what we use in most human communication. Principally, we use spoken language when Christian people assemble to encounter the One who can take your speech away. There are, to be sure, times when people are speechless, when they have thoughts, yearnings, and concerns, that are "too deep for words." Yet, as

3

preachers and leaders of public prayer and worship, we have a responsibility to speak when others cannot. Our job is to search for words that will draw people into an encounter with God and give expression to deeply held concerns. We trust that God will aid us in our weakness and give us something more than sighs to use in proclaiming God's promise and presence. What we are given are symbols that enable us to articulate ineffable things. There are also skills we can acquire that will assist us in the task of expressing matters of the heart. Finding appropriate language for preaching and leading in public prayer and worship is the subject of this book. Our first task will be to look at the discursive nature of language, the nondiscursive nature of art, and to consider the aesthetic responsibility of those whose role it is to speak of things too deep for words.

SYMBOLS TO REMIND US

When people express themselves, whether verbally, through gesture, or artistic media, they use symbols. The symbols employed can be anything designated to convey meaning: a word, a letter, a musical note, a patch of color, a movement, a design. Some symbols have no direct referent or particular meaning. The letter "q," as it stands alone, refers to nothing in particular and conveys no meaning until it is found in relationship with other letters or is assigned meaning in a certain context. The musical tone "A" (the tone produced at 440 vibrations per second) or the color brown also have no particular referents or meanings in isolation. Some symbols do have agreed-on referents and generally mean certain things. The word "dog" means a particular kind of house pet, and a picture of a dog refers to the same animal.

If a person wished to express a singular idea, say a cat, the person could simply say "cat" or show a photograph of a cat. Or that person could begin to place symbols together in order to make reference to the idea. For example, the person could choose to use patches and lines of brown paint, so placed on a page as to resemble the shape of a cat. The resulting picture, then, would be a combination of symbols that are worked together to give reference to an idea.

But pictures, as symbols or combinations of symbols, have a limitation in that they cannot represent configurations of ideas. As a static combination of lines, color forms, patterns, and shapes, a picture represents what might be called a frozen idea in that it does not unfold developing aspects of meaning. Even when the picture contains design elements that seem to move and have force and direction, the picture can only represent a given state of an artist's ideas. When a more elaborate thought is to be expressed, we rely on symbols that do have referents and meaning.

For such expression we use verbal symbols, or words. Words each have a particular agreed-on meaning or range of meanings, and in language we string them together in order to render the expression of an idea. Even though an idea may be something that occurs to a person as a full and complex array of thought in an instant, the expression of that idea needs to take time. It takes a while for a person to string words together as thought and bring them forth as utterance. This process is known as discourse. Discursiveness is that property of language that causes us to spin out strings of words to give verbal expression to our thoughts.[1]

The use of language is a particularly good way to give expression to complex ideas. Words, as verbal symbols each with its own meaning or range of meanings, can be strung together in countless combinations. The particular elements of meaning represented by each of the words are drawn together in combinations of meaning. As each word is uttered or read, its meaning adds itself to or brings modification to the meaning of the other words that relate to it in a sentence. Each sentence, in turn, represents certain aspects of a larger idea and adds itself to the unfolding meaning of the whole discourse. This is the way we typically articulate thoughts, whether they are elementary or elaborate, complete or developing, static or changing. Except for the restrictions of grammar, there is no limit to the arrangement of words that can be employed in our discourse. And there is no limit to the number of ideas that can be articulated by this common means.

Consequently, the use of discourse is our principal means of expressing ourselves. From the infant's first "Mama" to Stephen Hawking's explanations of the mysteries of the universe, language suffices to give expression to our thoughts, needs, wants, and understandings. When we speak or write, our intentions are stated. When we listen or read, we apprehend the intentions of others. When we engage in conversation, complex arrays of ideas, inspirations, problems, concerns, discoveries, uncertainties, and insights are exchanged. And as these ideas are shared, they are also shaped and understood. Discourse is a powerful mode of human communication, and language is a highly useful tool.

Yet language has a limitation. There are certain kinds of expression for which words fail us. These have to do with the subjective experience of the inner life. It is difficult to put into words the elements of experience that come to us through sensory channels and that derive from our affections. "How are you feeling?" someone might ask us and we might attempt to use language to give an answer. "Fine, thank you" or "Not very well" might give a general sense of our condition, but it will not indicate with any depth or accuracy the state of our being. Or we might give a more detailed account of our feelings: "I am physically well, yet tired from overwork, hungry, and amused at the ironies of life." Still, such an accounting does not express the range of emotion, the levels of sensory experience, or the depth of feeling that we experience at any given moment in life. Mere discourse is inadequate for the expression of life's deepest sensitivities. Philosopher Susanne K. Langer explains it this way:

> Everybody knows that language is a very poor medium for expressing our emotional nature. It merely names certain vaguely and crudely conceived states, but fails miserably in any attempt to convey the ever-moving patterns, the ambivalences and intricacies of inner experience, the interplay of feelings with thoughts and impressions, memories and echoes of memories, transient fantasy, or its mere runic traces, all turned into nameless, emotional stuff.[2]

Here, as people of faith, and particularly as those who preach the Word and lead God's people in rites of public worship and prayer, we encounter a problem. For in worship we are concerned with things that affect us deeply. As Philipp Melanchthon, the early German reformer, put it,

> ... through the Word and the rite God simultaneously moves the heart to believe and take hold of faith. . . . As the Word enters through the ears to strike the heart, so the rite itself enters through the eyes to move the heart.[3]

Worship deals, as Charles Bartow has said, with the "deepest mysteries of faith and life,"[4] matters that are so integrated into the core our being as to be "soul-deep."[5]

Of course, things of the soul are not divorced from things of the mind. Frank Burch Brown points out that the soul, or the "self as a whole," consists of the distinguishable but inseparable elements of the body and the heart, as well as the mind.[6] To be sure, an element of faith exists that deals directly with cognitive functions. There are concepts, ideas, and doctrines relating to the Christian faith that need to be taught and need to be understood by the believer. For the exposition of such elements of the faith, discourse is the most direct means of expression. Creedal formulas, catechetical material, theological insights, historical reports, and the like can be conveyed readily through the use of literal speech. But for articulating those aspects of the faith that relate more directly to our sensory perceptions or for speaking suasively in order to transform hearts and change lives, mere discourse is less effective. Whereas we can speak literally to one another of the tenets of our belief, how can we relate what a relationship with our Creator or with Jesus Christ can mean to us? How can we speak of the joy of salvation, one's gratitude for grace, a sense of wonder at the incarnation, one's guilt over being sinful, the shame of the crucifixion, or the peace that passes all understanding? And how can we speak of life's circumstances as they are experienced within and addressed by faith in Christ: the death of a parent, the birth of a child, the dawning of spring, the discovery of an illness, or the association of friends? Further, how can we speak to God in public prayer of a worshiping assembly's heartfelt needs? How can we put into words their fears, longings, gladness, remorse, pain, or praise? Sometimes words fail us and we are left to rely on the Spirit who intercedes for us with sighs too deep for words.

Such inspired sighs may indeed be our best mode of prayer at times, especially when praying privately. When our own thoughts or longings are beyond words, that the Spirit supplies our prayer by nondiscursive means is a gift of grace. But, as preachers and worship leaders, we need to speak and pray publicly. And we need to express ourselves in such a way that others are moved by our speech or drawn to prayer and praise along with us. How can we who require the use of language to perform our public responsibilities express ourselves in such a way as to affect others and reach them at the level at which faith resides? Where discursive symbols fail, another kind of symbol is necessary. For such expression, nondiscursive, or presentational, symbols are needed.

PRESENTATIONAL SYMBOLS

Presentational symbols are different from discursive symbols in that they do not present their constituent elements successively, as in the stringing together of words in language. Rather, they are presented simultaneously as in a picture, where all the elements work together at the same time to articulate some idea of the artist. Areas of light, shade, and color have no meaning in isolation. But, in a picture, they acquire symbolic meaning as they work together to compose a visual object that represents an artist's ideas.

What do these presentational symbols express? They express something of the experience of life that is known by the artist. Whereas pictures cannot express complex arrays of thought, they can capture and present aspects of the artist's feelings that can be seen and assimilated by those who view the picture. Pictures, especially those that are well made, can present forms of human feeling, or what Langer calls sentience. As she states it, presentational symbols

> bear a close logical similarity to the forms of human feeling—forms of growth and of attenuation, flowing and slowing, conflict and resolution, speed, arrest, terrific excitement, calm, or subtle activation and dreamy lapses—not joy and sorrow perhaps, but the poignancy of either and both—the greatness and brevity and eternal passing of everything vitally felt. Such is the pattern, or logical form, of sentience. . . .[7]

Imagine what happens when you view a great painting. You enter into a communication with the artist and begin to know something of his or her sensory and affective experience. The feelings you recognize through the art are difficult to express verbally. But they inhere in the work and, through it, a bridge is built that connects the artist's experience to your own inner life.

Another form of presentational, or nondiscursive, symbol is music. In music, an artist's ideas are given the form of sounds in time. The particular symbolic elements that constitute music—notes, chords, motifs, and rests—have no significance by themselves. Yet, in the composition, the parts work together and the whole is given to the ear as a presentation that exposits some idea of the composer.

As with pictures, music symbolizes that which words cannot express. Music may even incorporate language, as in song or opera, yet it articulates far more than the actual denotation of the words among the constituent elements of the work. Singing a hymn, for example, has a different impact on a worshiping assembly than does merely reciting its words. The singing of words and music together creates additional levels of meaning and brings to mind added associations. These may have to do with the satisfaction of singing in harmony with others, memories of singing a particular hymn at family gatherings, or the sense of being connected to believers from another culture from which the music derives. These are associations that come to individual participants in the singing that are neither expressed in the text of the hymn nor necessarily spoken of by members of the assembly. Yet they are present associations and part of the experience that occurs when music is joined to words.

Words alone do not even suffice to explain or describe a piece of music. Although one may use language to describe a given composition, it would be impossible to give a sense of the movement, power, and impact of the piece without letting it be heard for itself. Neither could one use language to speak of the range and subtlety of the emotions of the artist as demonstrated in the performance. Music does what language cannot: It gives articulation to those elements of experience that are ineffable.

Such things are known by those who sing. Several years ago, as director of a church choir, I had the opportunity to lead the group on a singing tour to Hungary. The tour occurred shortly after this former member of the Communist Bloc had broken away from Soviet control and was drawing its first breaths of freedom. Our tour objective was to share a sense of Christian unity with fellow believers in Hungary through music and to learn something of their experience with and struggle for the faith. As a way of providing our audiences with a sense of our own experience with the faith, we chose a repertoire that consisted almost entirely of American songs sung in English. Although we did not share a common language, it was hoped that our music would communicate beyond words. Throughout the tour, as we read the looks on the faces of our listeners and as we listened to comments from those with whom we could speak, we learned that our hope was met. But the most poignant indication that music communicated beyond words came when we sang one song in Hungarian.

We had chosen to close our concerts by singing the Hungarian national hymn, to the tune HIMNUSZ. Although we could not understand the words of the text we had learned, our guide helped us understand that the words were a prayer for peace. They spoke of great historic suffering by the Hungarian people. Indeed, the prayer suggested that the people felt they had already suffered sufficiently for ages to come. Their national hymn is a prayer that God grant them respite.

At the close of our first concert, we began to sing our listeners' prayer. Slowly, as they recognized its opening strains, the audience began to rise and to sing with us. As they sang, for many, especially the old, tears began to form and fall from their eyes. The combination of the stirring melody, the strong words, and their associations with this hymn born of lifetimes of faithfulness and desperation gave way to founts of passion. In response, many of the choir were stirred by the moment, and soon, nearly all were weeping as we sang together. Those who shared that experience knew that it was no mere sentimental display, but a moment when the vehicle of song became the conveyance for a shared understanding of faith. Although its words were not mutually understood, one people's prayer had become the bridge to another culture and had generated a moment when choir and audience were joined in the spirit of Christian unity.

Beyond musical and pictorial forms, there are many other modes of presentational symbol. They include sculpture, photography, film, dance, and many others. In a word, they include all forms of art.

In creating a work of art, an artist selects and manages the arrangement of elemental forms according to what Langer calls the "logical rightness and necessity of selection."[8] The artist is one who uses knowledge, skill, and inspiration[9] to select and manipulate the elements of his or her medium that best articulate an aesthetic idea.

These elemental symbols combine to make works of art, which present ideas that words could not, in themselves, express. How frustrating it is for a sculptor or composer to be asked what his or her work means. Such naive inquiry suggests that the nature of what the artist conceived could be put into words, if only the artist chose to do so; that the fullest and best understanding of an artist's work could be arrived at not simply by perceiving what the artist had to say presentationally in the work but by careful and thoroughgoing explanation of the particular referents of the elements of the work. This, of course, is not the way art works. In fact, the artist, if he or she were to attempt to indulge such questioning, would be hard pressed in the use of language to give fuller expression to the affective ideas that gave birth to the work of art. Nor would hearing such an explanation be the same as viewing or hearing the work. To enter into the mind and heart of the artist, one must enter into the artist's work and embrace what is presented there by virtue of the combinations of symbols that are arranged so as to articulate some idea that moved the artist to create it. Philosopher John Dewey goes so far as to suggest that

> if all meanings could be adequately expressed by words, the arts of painting and music would not exist. There are values and meanings that can be expressed only by immediately visible and audible qualities, and to ask what they mean in the sense of something that can be put into words is to deny their existence.[10]

Words and explanations simply cannot take the place of art. Consider the following description of the performance of "Mambo wa ku denga," a sacred song sung in an African service of worship:

> During the chanting, the rhythmic shape of the song is transformed as worshipers put increasing emphasis on strongly accented beats. . . . While the rhythm is accentuated, the harmonies of the chorus tighten. The loose collection of voices becomes a tight, single unit. The overall effect is hypnotic. The rhythmic and harmonic ramifications push the singers into a state of maximum spiritual involvement. As the chant proceeds, individuals moan, yodel, and insert *ngoma* [vocal sounds which imitate drumming] . . . and glossalalic utterances. The entire congregation sways to the rhythm.[11]

As you read the vivid description of the performance of this song, you get a sense of the mood of the assembly and the rhythm and drive of the music. But reading these words is no substitute for experiencing the performance in person. Whereas it seems to be a satisfactory depiction of the aesthetic moment, reading it is hardly satisfying and leaves us wanting for the opportunity to gain firsthand experience with the hypnotic power of the performance.

Because there are many forms of art, there are many types of elemental symbols that are used to create works of art. Painters use line, shape, color, texture, and pattern to create their work. Sculptors use shape, contour, depth, and shadow to produce a statue. Musicians use combinations of tone, harmony, rhythm, rest, duration, and tempo to make a song or a symphony. And writers use words to create poems, plays, novels, songs, and sermons. But how can words serve both as discursive symbols in literal uses of language and as presentational symbols in artistic forms? This question lies at the heart of this project and will be addressed later in this chapter as we consider the poetic nature of preaching and the language of worship.

ART AND THE WORLD OF FEELING

Philosophy has long struggled with the question of meaning in art. From Plato to the postmodernists, writers have considered such issues as the nature of creativity and aesthetic inspiration, audience responsiveness to works of art, and what artists are trying to communicate in their making. Although theories of the function and meaning of art differ greatly, what most philosophical investigations hold in common is that art has something to do with the expression of things that are part of the affective pattern of human experience.[12] Langer defines art quite simply: "Art is the creation of forms symbolic of human feeling."[13] Or, more elaborately, Hans Küng says that art is

> a great symbol . . . a symbol which . . . can remind us as human beings of the great heritage of the past, the future still to come, of the meaning, value, and dignity of our life here and now; a symbol that can rouse our passion for freedom and truthfulness, our hunger for justice and love, our yearning for fellowship, reconciliation, and peace; a symbol which may perhaps enable us to perceive something of what "involves us unconditionally," the still hidden, incomprehensibly great mystery around us. . . .[14]

As the symbol of human emotion, art is not simply the stimulation of human feeling. Nor is it the expression of the feelings that happen to beset the artist at the moment of artistic inspiration. It is, rather, the expression of what the artist knows about the inner life; the presentation of the artist's imagination of human feeling.[15] For example, a composer may capture a certain mood in his or her music, such as somber, excited, martial, or majestic. Yet the composer doesn't create such a mood only when he or she is personally in that emotional state of being. The composer writes the music and renders a recognizable mood because of what the composer knows about life's tempers and humors. The music is created by virtue of the composer's skill at selecting and arranging the right and necessary musical symbols that will accomplish the presentation. These symbols combine, when played, to render what is understood by listeners as a certain kind of mood. The mood, then, is perceived to be a part of the composition and it inheres in the work itself. Likewise, a painter does not paint only according to the personal feelings of the moment. Having lived, observed, and incorporated human experience into the treasury of his or her affective memory, the painter draws episodes out of this storehouse of ideas and presents them through artistic symbols as forms of human emotion.

From the perspective of the observer of a work of art, at least two perceptions are gained. The first is that the observer is acquainted with something new, something of the way that the artist perceives the forms and patterns of life.[16] Janet Walton refers to this as the "revelatory" function of art.[17] Romano Guardini gives an example of how this works in visual art:

> The tree on the canvas is not like that outside in the field. It is not "there" at all, but is placed, seen, felt as filled with the mystery of existence within the confines of the representation. The painter has given form to it in his vision and expressed his image in the external structure of lines and colors on the canvas in such a way that it can also emerge in the imagination of the person who contemplates this structure.[18]

The revelatory function of art is also at work in literature, as demonstrated by Northrup Frye:

> You wouldn't go to Macbeth to learn about the history of Scotland— you go to it to learn what a man feels like after he's gained a kingdom and lost his soul. When you meet a character such as Micawber in Dickens, you don't feel that there must have been a man Dickens knew who was exactly like this: you feel like there's a bit of Micawber in almost everybody you know, including yourself. Our impressions of human life are picked up one by one, and remain for most of us loose and disorganized. But, we constantly find things in literature that suddenly coordinate and bring into focus a great many impressions.[19]

In the same way, the revelatory function of art is at work in liturgical settings. When one looks at statues or stained-glass images of Jesus in places of worship, the observer perceives not an accurate representation or likeness of the historical figure but an understanding of the artist's conceptions about how the Christ would appear. The observer also takes in something of the artist's feelings associated with who Jesus is, his place in history, his connection to the faith, his relationship to the artist and to humanity, his relationship to God, and so forth.

The second perception that the observer gathers when encountering art has to do with resonance, whereby the work creates a connection between the audience and the artist. As Walter Ong has shown in *The Presence of the Word*, resonance is the capacity that allows for that which is interior to one person (or object) to reciprocate with that which is interior to another person (or object).[20] Just as a piano sounding the tone low "E" causes the low "E" string on a nearby bass violin to sound in sympathy (or perhaps, more accurately, in symphony), the sound of one person speaking communicates a sympathetic understanding in his or her listeners. In art, the medium of resonant communication can be auditory or visual. Aesthetic resonance occurs when that which is interior to the artist is communicated symbolically and presentationally through the artistic medium and is recognized and assimilated by that which is interior to the observer. In other words, art creates a vital sense of recognition in which the observer resonates with those emotive qualities of the artist as they inhere in the work of art.

This quality of aesthetic resonance is certainly at work in the arts of worship. In speaking of the poetry of Christian creeds, Geoffrey Wainwright has said that their poetry is able to speak "transhistorically, transculturally, and transpersonally."[21] This power of poetry in the creeds enables worshipers today not just to gain access to information about the faith but to join their hearts in solidarity with those ancient believers who long ago penned the words we now recite. Another example of aesthetic resonance at work in worship is found in the use of hymns. When a hymn sounds joyful or funereal, the listener is recognizing and resonating with the composer's sense of joyfulness or somberness, as these feelings relate to life in the faith. Such feelings are brought forth by virtue of the musical symbols that the composer selects and organizes into a melody and harmonization. To borrow the psalmist's image, "deep calls to deep" (Ps. 42:7) through the arts of worship, and the interiors of artists and audiences are connected.

Another aspect of aesthetic resonance is that it can combine in layers of connectivity. When a person listens to Beethoven's *Sonate Pathétique* played by a single pianist, he or she resonates not only with the feelings of the composer that gave inspiration to the piece but also with the feelings of the pianist who renders the piece according to individual interpretation. When a person listens to Bach's *Magnificat in D*, the listener is drawn not only into connection with the composer, but with the original author of the text and the feelings that gave rise to her utterance. In addition, there is simultaneous connection made between the listener and the instrumentalists who play the work, the chorus and soloists who sing it, and the conductor who provides his or her own personal interpretation in the performance of the piece. If the work of art is a hymn, there is a similar combining of layers of connectivity between the author of the text, the composer of the tune, the arranger of the tune, the accompanist who plays the hymn, and the individuals who join together in worship to sing it.

Language, too, can have the power of resonance. As Ong has demonstrated, the spoken word is the greatest key to interiority between people.[22] Yet, due to language's discursive limitation, it cannot create a connection between the most vital aspects of human interiority unless it has a presentational quality. What kind of language has the power to be not merely discursive, but presentationally symbolic at the same time? This felicitous union occurs in language that is artistically wrought. The common term for it is poetry.

LANGUAGE AS POETRY

How can language, which is discursive, overcome the limitation of being unable to communicate that which is soul deep? How can mere words function for us when our feelings are too deep for words? Writers and speakers who achieve such vital communication are artists and they use language in nondiscursive ways. Whether novelists, essayists, historians, lyric poets, playwrights, or preachers, artistic communicators use language that is not simply literal, but figurative. Such writers are poets. To understand how poetry works presentationally, we turn to look more carefully at one of the aesthetic theories that we have already briefly visited, that of Susanne K. Langer.[23]

The function of language, Langer says, is twofold:[24] to convey information and to stimulate feelings and attitudes in a listener. A poem may do both. Poetic criticism has tended to understand poetry in light of those functions by asking, "What is the author trying to say?" and "What is the poet trying to make us feel?"[25] Langer suggests that the most critical initial question needs to be, "What has the poet made and how did he [or she] make it?"[26] Langer's concept of artistic semblance provides the answer.

All art, she says, has the quality of semblance or illusion. It is a quality that is similar to that which happens when someone is engrossed in an interesting conversation or event. One's attention is drawn into the object of interest to such an extent that the person becomes unaware of peripheral circumstances. Certainly, a practical awareness of one's surroundings may be there, but only in a secondary position. This happens in perceiving art, as well. When a person is drawn into consideration of a painting or a symphony, that person loses awareness of the fact that she is standing in a gallery or that he is seated in a concert hall. The allure of the picture or the music is greater than any distraction that competes with the art. This is due not to any special gifts of the percipients for concentration. Rather, it is a property of the work of art itself, which, if it functions successfully, detaches itself from its surroundings.[27] "Every real work of art has a tendency to appear thus dissociated from its mundane environment."[28] Langer describes this property as an impression of "otherness" from reality. The work of art has the impression of an illusion enfolding it. Even where the element of representation is absent, where nothing is imitated or feigned, as in a textile pattern, a piece of pottery, a building, or a sonata, this air of illusion, of being sheer image, exists as forcibly as in the most deceptively accurate picture.[29]

Returning to the questions about poetry, what has the poet made? The poet has made an illusion, the semblance of something that is as complete as that created by the visual artist on canvas or the composer of music. And how has the poet made such an illusion? "The poet," says Langer, "uses discourse to create an illusion, a pure appearance, which is a nondiscursive symbolic form."[30] The poet is certainly using a discursive symbolic form by means of which the poet's ideas are strung out in the form of language. But when the poet has finished his or her work, the poem functions in a nondiscursive manner. The particular words that the poet selects and their particular denotations and connotations may have little actual connection to the feelings that are nondiscursively presented in a poem. Consider the example of a poet who describes the rise of the sun in rich verbal imagery. The poem, if it is successful, does two things. Discursively, it gives a description of a recurring event that has been witnessed by countless generations of people. Nondiscursively, the poem stands as a work of art that functions to acquaint the audience with something it has not known before, namely, the poet's ideas about the emotions associated with watching a beautiful sunrise. The poet at no time uses words to talk about emotions or to speak of how sun watchers feel. Yet the audience is unmistakably moved by a good poem to perceive something of the feelings of the author as they resonate within. Thus, the poet has created an illusion. The illusion is not a sunrise or a pretend sunrise. The illusion is a form through which is symbolized the semblance of those feelings that might be associated with people who are moved by watching a sunrise.

To speak in general terms, what is the illusion that any poetic semblance creates? It is the illusion of life, or what Langer calls, "virtual life." "Poetry," she says, "creates a virtual 'life,' or, as is sometimes said, 'a world of its own.' . . . A world created as an artistic image is given us to look at, not to live in."[31] It is never real life that the poet creates, but a presentational symbol, a form that works to present a semblance of human life and human emotions.

As an example of how this works, let us examine how the qualities of illusion and virtual life are at work in the poetry of the Bible. Consider the words of Psalm 121:

> I lift up my eyes to the hills—from where will my help come?
> My help comes from the Lord, who made heaven and earth.
> He will not let your foot be moved; he who keeps you will not slumber.
> He who keeps Israel will neither slumber nor sleep.
> The Lord is your keeper; the Lord is your shade at your right hand.
> The sun shall not strike you by day, nor the moon by night.
> The Lord will keep you from all evil; he will keep your life.
> The Lord will keep your going out and your coming in from this time on
>   and forevermore.

In this example, what has the psalmist made? The psalmist has used discourse to create an illusion. The reader does not take on the actual dread or relief of the writer nor live out the circumstances that give rise to the psalm's creation.

But the illusion of those circumstances is there. The psalm's message could be summarized: There is the sense of a person in trouble looking to the hills for aid, yet realizing that true assistance comes not from human resources but from God. Then, reciting a list of figures, the psalmist paints a picture of a God who is able to hold us fast, who is ever attentive, who sustains us, and who protects us for all time. This two-sentence summary gives the literal sense of the psalm in a strictly discursive sense. Yet it does not capture the power of the strong images nor render the assurance of the writer who is able to create for us an illusion of real life. In this illusion, people of faith will recognize the pattern of real things: humanity's need for divine guardianship and the serenity that comes from knowing that God protects and provides for us. Although the writer doesn't explicitly say that we should find comfort in God's presence and care or take delight in a God who is ever watchful, these things are understood. In fact, they are more than understood because the serenity of the author resonates with the inner knowledge of serenity in the reader; the peace of the author becomes the agent of peace in the reader. Although, strictly speaking, the psalm is discourse, due to its presentational quality it transforms the reader. The reader not only learns something new, something of the writer's experience with trust in God, but also assimilates that trust and knows it, to a degree, for him- or herself.

As it has been suggested above and will be more fully demonstrated in succeeding chapters, preaching is also a form of poetic discourse. The same can be said of public prayer and, indeed, all language that is used in the leadership of public worship. In the chapters that follow, the poetic nature of these elements of liturgical expression will be considered more fully. For the present, we turn our attention to the question of how the artistic quality of illusion functions more generally in worship.

WORSHIP AS VIRTUAL EXPERIENCE

We have seen, in considering the presentational quality of poetry, how art has a quality of illusion enfolding it. It has, as Janet Walton says, a characteristic that "reaches beyond the boundaries of tangible realities."[32] In Langer's theory of art, she has defined classifications of illusion as a means of identifying the differences between categories of art. She argues that, just as poetry exhibits a unique kind of illusion, every form of art has its own kind of semblance that reflects some aspect of human experience. The "virtual life" depicted in poetry is a result of its ability to present the semblance of human experience in verbal form. In painting, where what is being viewed is merely a flat surface covered with paint, the viewer perceives the dimensional illusion that he or she is looking *into* the painting and seeing what Langer calls "virtual space." Music, as moving forms of sound unfolding in time, has, she says, the illusion of "virtual time." Similarly, literature, which depicts realms of events that are presented as lived and completed, gives a sense of "virtual memory." And drama, given that performances unfold in the immediate moment and draw observers into consideration of that which is to come, creates a sense of "virtual future." In the force and movement of dance, she sees the illusion of "virtual power." Although Langer dealt only with certain art forms, she invited her readers to apply her theory to forms outside her purview. Taking up this invitation, let us consider how her theory applies to the art of worship.

If worship is art, what is the illusion that worship creates, which, when sustained, allows it to serve as the symbol of human feeling? One writer has given an arguable answer to this question. In *More than Meets the Eye*, Patrick Collins uses Langer's aesthetic theory to demonstrate that liturgical ritual resembles the virtual life of poetry, the virtual future of drama, the virtual power of dance, and the virtual time of music. These are, he says, analogs to, or parables of, ritual activity. Collins suggests that as a form of art itself, worship exhibits its own unique quality of semblance, which he identifies as "virtual presence."[33] By this he means that when people worship, they engage in ritual activity that resembles artistic forms and that creates for worshipers the illusion of being in God's presence.

> Such artistic forming of the elements of worship takes bread, wine, oil, gesture, word, sound and assembly and gives them a new embodiment. These isolated things are set free from their normal condition and reordered into a new constellation of elements called ritual. They are no longer "things" but appearance or semblance. This new semblance or illusion is what is immediately given for perception.[34]

The forms of these things are used "to create the virtual image of Presence which is," he argues, "the primary illusion of ritual art."[35]

Collins's category of semblance seems unsatisfactory for two reasons. The first is that there is no possibility for the generalization of his theory to other forms of ritual. There are certain elements of similarity between the rituals of worship and numerous other kinds of ritual. Yet when people are engaged in nonreligious rituals, they have no expectation of a divine encounter nor the realization of any virtual presence of God. For example, the opening ceremonies of the Olympic Games are similar in many ways to the religious rituals of worship. There is an assembly of people, a procession of participants, musical performances, addresses to the assembly by speakers, and climactic, almost sacramental moments, such as when the torch is lighted. Like worship, the Olympic opening ceremonies are also artistic. The ceremonies typically include drama, dance, music, and visual artistry. Yet there is no expectation in these events of a divine encounter or a realization of "virtual presence" in such a secular setting. In other words, the quality of "virtual presence" cannot be generalized to other ritual forms in the way that Langer's categories of semblance can be generalized to related art forms. Whereas the category of virtual life can be found both in secular poetry and in preaching, the "virtual presence" of liturgical ritual cannot be found in secular ritual.

The second problem with Collins's claim that "virtual presence" is the primary illusion of liturgical ritual is that when people gather for worship, they do so not in the virtual presence of God but in God's *real* presence. It is not an illusion of God to which worshipers pray, but a present, divine participant to whom petitions are addressed. Likewise, God is present in the Word, the preaching, the sacraments, and even in the assembly of the local configuration of the body of Christ. Were God's presence only an illusion, worship might be art, but it would be nothing more. It would hold no more theological significance than viewing religious art at the Louvre or the Hermitage. Indeed, it is God's actual presence in worship that distinguishes it from all other ritual. Even if the liturgical ritual takes on sparse form, as in Quaker worship, or unique form, as in spontaneous public prayer, it is the presence of God that makes such public ritual worship events. We trust that the divine presence is given just as it is promised in Matthew 18:20: "For where two or three are gathered in my name, I am there among them." "The gathering itself furnishes the matrix," says Walter Ong, "the womb for [Christ's] coming, as Mary's body once did. If the group calls and waits on him, he is there."[36]

If "virtual presence" is not the primary illusion of worship, is there a more appropriate category that can account for the range of illusions that worship incorporates and that can be generalized to other forms of ritual? Only one answer seems tenable: virtual experience. This is a category of illusion that is broad enough to encompass the illusions of life, time, space, power, memory, and future that correlate to the forms of poetry, music, visual art, dance, literature, and drama that are the constituent elements of worship and other ritual. In life, numerous elements constitute each individual's personal experience. They include feelings, memory, the passing of time, a knowledge of history as well as one's own personal history, a sense of space and shape, movement, hopes, expectations for the future, faith, and so on. Because worship is made up of so many artistic forms, each of these aspects of personal experience can be symbolized and captured in a virtual representation by one or more of the arts that constitute worship. Therefore, the sum of these illusionary elements of worship yields a quality of *virtual experience*. The same can be said of other forms of ritual. They, too, are filled with the semblance of virtual experience in that they represent ranges of human experience through multiple artistic forms.

How is virtual experience exhibited in worship? The elements of worship are not created to duplicate everyday existence. The virtual life found in a sermon is not the same as the real experience of life. The virtual space of religious paintings, sculpture, or stained-glass windows is not real space that can be measured and inhabited. Likewise, the virtual time, power, future, and history of worship are not the same as the time, power, future, and history of genuine personal existence. Yet all of these elements make up the experience of a person and, in worship, they are represented in such a way that the worshiper recognizes them as illusions of genuine experience. It is not real experience that is presented in worship, but ideas about human experience or symbols of human experience. Thus, worship is a complex of symbols that reflects the breadth of human experience and exhibits a semblance of its range. Part of the range of that life experience is the genuine encounter with the Divine that is known by believers, especially as they meet God in worship.

How is God met and known in worship? A large part of that encounter takes place in the dialogue that occurs between those who gather and God. We now turn our attention to consider the dialogical nature of worship and the theological imperative that calls for that dialogue to be nondiscursive.

WORSHIP AS AESTHETIC DIALOGUE

When Christians gather for worship, they engage in a dialogue that runs in several directions. God speaks to the people; people speak to God; people speak to one another.[37] In each of these avenues of communication, sentient issues are at stake. We listen to God for assurance, correction, forgiveness, and hope. We speak to God of yearnings, concerns, burning needs, passions, joys, fears, and gratitude. We seek from one another a sense of community, support, forgiveness, and love. Because much of what yearns for expression in these dialogical movements is too deep for words, we rely on the use of presentational forms to communicate that which would otherwise be inexpressible. Without an aesthetic dimension to the dialogue of worship, the assembly of believers might well simply pitch together in the heaving of that Spirit-borne sigh. But artistic elements are part of the fabric of this web of intercommunication.

As God addresses the assembly, we see aesthetic principles at work in two ways. The first has to do with the way that God encounters us in worship. Through prayer, praise, thanksgiving, the Word, and the sacraments, worshipers meet and interact with the Divine. The striking thing about this encounter is that it cannot be known empirically. God's presence cannot be seen or measured, calculated or quantified in any way. Yet worshipers trust in that presence and know it to exist not only because of the promise given, but the presence felt. Although it cannot be demonstrated or proven, worshipers know the presence of God as God's peace settles over them or as the Spirit challenges them or brings them to a new insight into their faith. Whatever confidence a worshiper might have concerning God's presence in worship, it is an assurance that is born of the person's feelings rather than his or her reason. Knowledge of God's presence is not an intellectual perception but a sentient one. Moreover, not only is our perception of God a matter of the heart, so is God's perception of us. Paul tells us repeatedly (as in Rom. 5:5; 8:27; 10:9–10; 2 Cor. 1:22; 4:6) that faith resides in the heart and that God's knowledge of a person comes from searching his or her heart. Thus, when people meet God in worship and when God interacts with people in worship, the exchange is one that takes place at the soul-deep level of experience. If worship is indeed successful at engendering the divine encounter, then worship, as it consists of various forms of expression, is a complex of symbols that works at the level of human feeling. As we have seen, symbols that work in this way are known as art. In other words, *worship is art*. Yet some practitioners would argue that their forms of worship are not artistic and that they seek to avoid associating their worship with artistic forms. As Frank Burch Brown has reported, "thus, some Protestants attempt to do nothing other than proclaim the 'plain and simple truth' received from the Bible." Yet he goes on to say,

> aesthetic factors are involved even here where they are seldom recognized as such. The relatively unceremonious style of worship and pulpit rhetoric often associated with Free Church Protestantism has an aesthetic rhythm and impact of its own.[38]

That worship is, in this sense, an art not only explains why worship typically consists of aesthetic components, it also demonstrates that worship needs to be artful in order to enable the dialogue that occurs between God and believers.

This brings us directly to the second consideration of the ways that aesthetic principles are at work in the dialogue between Creator and creature in worship. When God speaks to us in worship, it is primarily through the reading of Scripture and the preaching of God's Word. Both of these rely on artistic measures. The Bible is rich with vivid imagery, evocative language, metaphor, and story. Even those aspects of Scripture that are intended merely to furnish the reader with information are often artistically rendered. Thus, as Brown reminds us, the story of Joseph's life as told in Genesis is art even though the actual historical experience of it was not.[39] Brown even suggests the possibility that the inelegant style of Paul's writing, with its rugged language and "audacious paradox," cannot be fully understood when read from a perspective devoid of aesthetic perception.[40]

Likewise, in the preaching of God's Word, the Bible's truth and its power to affect people's lives are rendered through aesthetic means. Like the scriptural writers, preachers use evocative language, metaphor, story, poetry, and narrative structure to speak the Word of God to people who assemble to hear it. Because of the potency of artistic symbols to address the psychological and spiritual depths of worshipers, preaching has the power to foster growth in faith and to transform lives.

The second orientation of the dialogue of worship is from people to God. Here, too, we see that aesthetic principles are at work in two ways. The first has to do with the human-divine resonance that occurs when people perform according to their nature.

In the first chapter of Genesis, we are told that human beings are created in the image of the Creator. There are numerous theological theories about what being created in God's image means. But one aspect of this is clear. Human beings have been created to be creative. Only God can create ex nihilo, of course, but humans have been given the ability to use imagination, skill, and craftsmanship in a way that no other animals have to build things, to devise theories, to express themselves, and to create art. All animals can procreate but only people can create. In this ability, we have been made to mirror divine creativity. This has been demonstrated throughout history. From early cave wall drawings to the most sophisticated nineteenth-century symphonic composition, humans have expressed themselves artistically. Because there is more to human experience than words can express, people have given themselves to artistic expression as the natural articulation of the ineffable aspects of their existence. Creating artistic expression is simply doing what humans have been created to do. Being creative, whether as an artist, artisan, or an imaginative worker, is fulfilling the essence of human capacity.

For this reason, worship has developed along aesthetic lines. People have designed the rituals of worship to be filled with artistic expression. Not only does artistic expression enable the articulation of the sentient experiences that are associated with one's faith, but it also enables people to experience a resonance with the Creator. God has created us and all that exists. In our imaginative response to God's creativity, we create forms of expression that reflect and resonate with God's creativity. We experience the fullness of being human in worship as we acknowledge our place as being nothing more than a part of God's creation, yet nothing less than the jewel of creation to whom God has given the ability to be creative. Thus, understanding that worship is art is simply to be aware that people are made in God's image and that, when assembled to celebrate our relationship with the Creator, we choose creative expressions to articulate our faith and to resonate with God's creativity.

A second aspect of being made in God's image is that we are made with the capacity for communicating with God. God speaks (through Word, sacrament, and sometimes, that still, small voice within) and we can listen. Likewise, we speak and God hears us. Thus, the orientation of the dialogue in worship is not only divine to human, but human to divine.

When people pray privately, they can use any form of communication to express their sentiments. One could speak to God aloud, or read aloud from written prayers or psalms. Perhaps the more common practice is to engage in silent patterns of thought that form themselves as analogs to speech. We may not simply say things in our heads the way we would speak them, but thought patterns often do follow the lines of spoken language. There are also times of prayer, as Paul has reminded us, when our concerns form in patterns that defy verbal articulation and we are given nothing more than sighs by which the Spirit conveys our plea. But there are other nonverbal possibilities as well. For example, a painter might render his or her expression of private praise through explosions of color and form on a canvas. Or a composer might render feelings of sorrow to God by offering them in composition. One thinks especially in this regard of the "Crucifixus" of Bach's *B Minor Mass*. Here in consummate tonal form is a wrenching depiction of sorrow from the heart of one who wrote both sacred and secular works as *soli Deo gloria*. Even though intended for public performance, such a work came from Bach's private life of faith and appears as much as a personal prayer as it does a public expression of his faith.

When people pray publicly, those forms of communication that serve for private prayer may not be effective. As we have said, when one prays alone, any form will do. When two people choose to pray together, some agreement as to form and style must be made: In which order will each speak? Will they fold or hold each other's hands? Where will the prayer take place? With only two people involved, such considerations can be agreed on with little delay. But when the number of those joining in prayer increases, more care must be given to matters of form, order, and style. The place and time of the prayer become a factor. It must also be decided who will lead in the prayer and how others will respond. When there are personal petitions, they take on a form that allows for others to participate in their appeal. In various settings, participants might agree to the acceptability of spontaneously crying out "Amen, sister." Or they might be trained to respond in unison with "In mercy hear us," or to sing the Taizé chant, "O Lord, hear our prayer." Similarly, the language used in public prayer needs to be crafted so as to draw the assembly into the activity of prayer and to speak of the needs and concerns of those gathered.

When public prayer is a part of worship, the language, form, and style of prayer become items of concern for worship leaders. They have the responsibility to create liturgical settings that involve all who gather, draw them together in unified activity, address them and their concerns at the level of soul-deep experience, and lead them to encounter the One who is present, yet unseen. If this is to be accomplished, the human-divine dialogue needs to assume, as we have seen, aesthetic form.

The third orientation in the dialogical structure of worship is from person to person. Here, too, we find aesthetic principles at work. This is evident in those aspects of worship that foster a sense of Christian unity among the many who assemble.

In the fourth chapter of Ephesians, the writer indicates that there is one Christian faith born of one Spirit, one body of Christ, one baptism, and one Lord. When Christians assemble in worship to experience that oneness in faith, it is worship's aesthetic nature that helps to foster such unity. Because people have diverse experiences with the faith and a variety of ways of understanding the Scriptures, worship is a medium that enables these various patterns of spiritual experience to be shared and incorporated by those present. A resonance exists between ministers and people, worship leaders and participants, musicians and listeners, composers and singers, preachers and listeners, visual artists and percipients. When people are engaged in worship, they participate in the aesthetic exchange that art creates. They are brought to an awareness of something new, something of the faith-related ideas and feelings of those who share and have historically shared their faith. A worshiper today is made aware of the faith experiences of those who long ago have written biblical literature and hymns, prayers, and creeds. Sermon listeners capture a conception of the preacher's feelings about a scriptural text and his or her sense of its application for life. Observers become aware of the spiritual perceptions of visual artists as they are presented in their work. Worship music engages listeners and participants and empowers them to resonate with the faith experiences of composers and performers. Songs and hymns enable singers to enter into solidarity with other worshipers as the music symbolizes the complex array of feelings associated with each individual's religious experience. In sum, the artistic nature of worship engenders a sense of the unity of faith as individual participants perceive and participate in the aesthetic activities that draw them together in cohesion and community.

ART FOR FAITH'S SAKE

In the mid-nineteenth century a philosophical shift occurred in the field of fine art. There was a backlash against what was considered to be a tyrannical understanding of the purpose of art. Conservative modernist painters believed that their work helped to improve the world by presenting images that reflected good moral values, virtuous behavior, Christian sentiments, and noble sacrifice.[41] But more progressive modernists saw the use of art in support of such political and religious ideals as restrictive. They developed ideas that challenged institutional authority, and they fostered art that was unfettered by political or societal expectation. The art of progressive modernists sought freedom from the rules of academic art and from the demands of the public. They claimed that art should not be produced for the public's sake, but for art's sake alone. The catchphrase of this movement was "art for art's sake."[42]

What we have seen in this chapter is that as art functions in worship, it serves as a means of expressing things that *are* important to the public (or at least, the worshiping public). Worship art is created not merely for the sake of creating beauty but in order to articulate forms of human experience that are too deep for words. The significance of art in worship is the connection it makes between the ones who create the works and the audience that perceives them, and the way that such connections teach, inspire, transform, and unite the assembly.

In looking specifically at the ways that language can be used poetically in worship, we have seen how preaching, public prayer, and the general language of worship leadership have the power to articulate things of the heart. In the same way, it could be shown that, through their powers of illusion, music, visual art, architecture, drama, and dance function in worship to express sentient things. As these individual forms of art work together, they combine to create a broad form of expression that assimilates each of these aesthetic elements. Just as in opera, where music, poetry, visual art, dance, and drama combine to develop a broader art form, so in worship the many forms of artistic expression combine to create an umbrella of aesthetic form.

Because worship, as a form of art, has the power to give expression to the ineffable elements of subjective experience and to deal with matters that are soul deep, it follows that preachers and worship leaders need to be aware of the artistic responsibility that is associated with their roles. If worship is not artful and worship leaders fail to execute their offices artistically, then worship runs the risk of failing to reach worshipers at their psychological and spiritual depths. Conversely, when worship is performed artistically, it serves the ministerial function of providing ritual form that is intrinsically connected to the feelings and experiences of those who gather. Artistically responsible worship also opens people's perceptions to the reception of something new and to resonation with the conceptions of others. The sense of artistic responsibility that accrues to worship leaders and preachers is suggested forcefully by Aidan Kavanagh:

> As does any art form, the liturgy gives enlarged room for imagination,
> for investment in and appropriation of values and for freedom. The
> difference between a liturgy which does this and one which does not
> is the difference between art and propaganda, between creation and
> exploitation.[43]

Whereas such an understanding of worship as art does not support the notion of "art for art's sake," it does agree with a phrase coined by art collector and church musician Jerry Evenrud: "art for faith's sake."[44] The arts of worship are created not merely for the sake of beauty and in freedom from human and institutional expectation. They are created for the sake of God's people in order to open hearts as well as minds; to touch people deeply, strengthen their faith, and evoke a transformation in their lives.

CONCLUSION

In this chapter we have seen how all human expression is symbolic, either discursively or presentationally, and how mere discourse is an insufficient conveyance for articulating the forms of human experience that are too deep for words. We have also seen how the use of presentational symbols, as they are rendered in forms of art, can give expression to those elements of subjective experience that are ineffable. Because faith and worship have to do with matters of the heart, it was shown that worship has and needs to have elements that are artistic. We next examined some theological implications relating to the aesthetic nature of worship as we considered its illusionary quality and its dialogical structure. Finally, a theological claim was made: that art is a significant and necessary part of worship, created for faith's sake to open both minds and hearts and to touch and change the lives of those who believe and assemble. In the next chapter, we will continue to focus on theological concerns as we move our attention to a consideration of the paradox of God's simultaneous presence and absence in worship. Pursuing the thesis that preachers and those who lead in public prayer and worship have an aesthetic responsibility, I will attempt to demonstrate the need for these ministers to express themselves in ways that disclose the hidden presence.

2

By Faith and Not by Sight

Although the doors were shut, Jesus came and stood among them and said, "Peace be with you." Then he said to Thomas, "Put your finger here and see my hands. Reach out your hand and put it in my side. Do not doubt but believe." Thomas answered him, "My Lord and my God!" Jesus said to him, "Have you believed because you have seen me? Blessed are those who have not seen and yet have come to believe."

John 20:26–29

To this point, we have discussed issues of symbol and artistic expression and demonstrated the need for the language of sermons, prayers, and worship leadership to be nondiscursive so that it might speak to spiritual depths and move people's hearts. We need presentational modes of expression if we are to find ways to speak to the issues of faith and life that are too deep for words. One of the elements of worship that is known at the soul-deep level is our encounter with God's presence. It is an unseen presence, yet one that is felt, trusted, and tangible in hidden ways. God comes to us in worship not merely as audience to our praise but as a dynamic presence performing acts of love. The purpose of this chapter will be to consider the issues of God's presence and performance in worship and to explore the need for preachers and worship leaders to perform their roles in ways that disclose the divine presence.

Who is present in worship? Those who assemble are the body of Christ, made up of people with differing roles and varying degrees of spiritual engagement. There are the *many* who come to participate in the songs and prayer, listen to the Word as read and preached, give assent to the community's place in baptism, be nourished by the Eucharist, and be sent out in service to Christ. Among them may be both the initiated and those inquiring into the faith; some, spiritually mature and well versed in the local patterns unfolding about them; others, newly initiated and still learning the forms, songs, and patterns of prayer. They will be people diverse in age, culture, and circumstance.

Also present in worship are the *few* with specialized roles. There may be people in the choir who lead the assembly and perform so as to draw the listeners into the interconnectedness that results from their musical expression. They may also include the trained laypeople who perform the ministerial functions of canting, accompanying music, reading Scripture, leading in prayer, and serving as acolytes, banner bearers, and crucifers. In more central roles, there are usually the preaching minister and the presiding minister (along with any who concelebrate as in Roman Catholic tradition).

These are the constituency of worship, people who are present to one another as the community of faith. But the list is incomplete, for they cannot gather as the people of faith unless the center and focus of that faith is also present. Worship cannot be godly, or God-pleasing, unless it is the gathering of God's people in the presence of God. Christian worship is the assembly and the active participation of the *many*, the *few*, and the *One*.

GOD'S PRESENCE IN WORSHIP

That God is present in worship is a subclass of the broader biblical belief that God is present in all things. Martin Luther expressed the idea with a sense of wonder:

> God is substantially present everywhere, in and through all creatures, in all their parts and places, so that the world is full of God and He fills all, but without His being encompassed and surrounded by it. . . . These are all exceedingly incomprehensible matters; yet they are articles of our faith and are attended clearly and mightily in Holy Writ. . . . For how can reason tolerate it that the Divine majesty is so small that it can be substantially present in a grain, on a grain, over a grain, through a grain, within and without, and that, although it is a single Majesty, it nevertheless is entirely in each grain separately? . . . And that the same Majesty is so large that neither this world nor a thousand worlds can encompass it and say: "Behold, there it is!"[1]

Luther's wonder lies in close parallel with that of a young friend of mine. In a confirmation class discussion of the First Article of the Apostles' Creed, this technically minded youth offered a less poetic but more scientifically astute insight: "Perhaps God is present everywhere and in all things as the most basic subatomic stuff that holds the atom together."[2] Although such a hypothesis is doubtlessly beyond the quantification of physical science, to take this figuratively is to perceive that God not only created all things but continues to be fundamentally attendant in and throughout the cosmos. This suggests both a transcendent and an immanent quality to the presence of God. It is a view shared by Ninian Smart, who said that "God's creative activity is not confined to his being there at the moment of creation; but he is present at the continuous creation of the world every day and every minute. . . ."[3] Smart couples this understanding of God's omnipresence with a conception that God can also be "multipresent," "present in varying degrees," and in "degrees of special presence."[4] This perception of God's omnipresence launches a trajectory which Geoffrey Wainwright follows in his book, *Doxology*, as he discusses the ways that God is present and active in the world and in the sacraments.[5] Following this path, we can see that the God who is omnipresent, but also capable of varying and special degrees of presence, is present in special ways in worship. The God who is in every grain and atom is even more present in the assembly of the body of Christ, in the Word, and in the sacraments.[6]

The knowledge of God's presence in worship is a common structural member in the framework of Judeo-Christian theology.[7] For ancient Jews, it was a point of rabbinical certification. The Mishnah declares: "If ten men sit together and occupy themselves with the Law, the divine presence rests among them, for it is written, God standeth in the congregation of God."[8] In early Christian times, God's presence was understood and proclaimed by those being brought into the faith who claimed "God is really among you."[9] And so we believe today, that as the few and the many gather to participate together in the rituals of Christian worship, the One is present and active.

PRESENCE AND PERFORMANCE

In the first chapter we spoke of the dialogical nature of worship and the three directions of that conversation. That the conversation crisscrosses in a three-fold pattern suggests that all participants are active in the dialogue. The people hear and respond to God's Word, the preacher and worship leaders speak to the people and to God in their behalf, and God speaks through Scripture and sermon. To put it in more artistic terms, all participants are performers in the liturgical dialogue.

The term *performance* is avoided in some liturgical circles because it suggests an entertainment quality that much Christian worship tries to avoid. For the choir or a soloist to perform a piece of music suggests that the assembly sits as an audience in mute and attentive appreciation of the musical presentation. For lectors to present their scriptural readings as oral interpretation of literature suggests that the delivery of the reading is for the enjoyment of the audience. With preachers who seem to be so animated and evocative as to perform in the pulpit, the suggestion is that they are merely acting and do not have something authentic to say. Those who lead public prayer with illustrious language are suspected of being like the hypocrites of Jesus' admonition who love to "stand and pray in the synagogues and at the street corners, so that they may be seen by others" (Matt. 6:5).

The concern over worship that is mere entertainment rather than engagement is valid.[10] The liturgical dialogue involves active participation by all present. But to shy away from matters of performance is to misunderstand the nature of the occurrent arts that make up worship. In any public form of expression there is a time of preparation, often known as rehearsal, and a time of presentation, usually known as performance. To perform in worship is simply to do what preachers and worship leaders train and prepare to do: to give public expression to musical, dramatic, dance, or discursive forms that make up the patterns of worship.

Performance-mindedness in worship is avoided for another reason. It implies that performers will draw undue attention to themselves and distract from the congregation's focus on more central issues. This concern is reinforced by preachers and worship leaders who use the pulpit and chancel to grandstand, demonstrating the magnificence of their abilities, techniques, or erudition. I received an early example of this in my first year of seminary. Our worship class met for a practice session in which we took turns chanting the "Kyrie." One of the students, we were to discover, had a magnificent baritone voice. As he stood confidently to chant the prayer, forth came an unexpectedly loud, ringing tone. "In peace, let us pray to the Lord!" he bellowed. It was followed by silence. We were supposed to respond "Lord, have mercy." But we could not sing. Some were overwhelmed and afraid to croak an inelegant response. Others of us were simply taken by the richness of his vocal quality and the cocksure presence before us. The class stopped still. Had it been an actual moment of congregational prayer, I trust there would have been a similar response, and the prayer for mercy would have been at least diverted and at worst supplanted by admiration for the cantor. Proper performance involves the use of judgment and humility. The grand, Shakespearean tone of Olivier's Hamlet is very different from that of his portrayal of the maniacal Nazi dentist Christian Szell in *Marathon Man*. One anticipates that Carreras would sing a child to sleep in a different tone than with which he sings "La Donna É mobile" in Verdi's *Rigoletto*. To suggest that preachers and worship leaders perform their roles well means that from the resources available to them they use those which, according to the logical rightness and necessity of selection, will advance their liturgical objectives.

Recently, several theologians have written of the performance aspects of worship and preaching. Rather than to be avoided, they have argued that there is much to be learned from the realms of performance. Richard Ward gives two helpful definitions of the word *performance*. It comes, he says, "from old French *par + fournir* which literally means to 'carry through to completion.'"[11] He holds that preachers are performers in that they bring to completion in the pulpit the message they have begun in the study. He also speaks of performance as "form coming through."

> Actors, oral interpreters, storytellers, and others who have an experiential understanding of performance processes perceive . . . that when an oral interpreter reads a poem aloud to an audience, the *form* of the poem comes through the speaker. When a storyteller tells a story, he or she allows the *form* of the story to "come through" in the telling. In the enactment of a play, the form of a character comes through the actor playing the role. Similarly, when you preach, the form of your sermon either comes through or does not come through your character, your body, your voice, the "individual, private miracle" that is your self *and* the part of you that is formed by the community.[12]

In a similar vein, Jana Childers argues that preaching is "performing the Word" and suggests that preachers can learn about their art by learning what actors know.[13] She also sees worship as theater. "Worship is about *all* of God's people performing—giving form to—their response to God."[14] Charles Bartow is another who argues for an awareness of performance sensitivities by preachers and worship leaders. "Theology, art, and technique . . . converge in any human performative enterprise," he says.[15] The Word of God is "God's self-performance," and our reading or speaking of it in worship is God's human speech given as "God's self-disclosure" in "performative events."[16] The purpose here is not to recapitulate these strong arguments in favor of performance awareness in worship, but to demonstrate that when the One, the many, and the few are present in worship, they are involved in a latticework of interconnected activity. Worship is not only the gathering but the active participation of all present.

That the few who lead worship are active, or performing, is clear. Those who read, preach, sing, and speak in their turn are performing in the sense of making the texts of liturgy, Scripture, sermon, and prayer come alive as enactment. Whether these texts are scripted or composed for the day, their form comes through in the way that they are sung or spoken. That the many who gather are active, or performing, is also known. Those in the assembly move together; sing together; recite prayers, creeds, and litanies; clap; shout out affirmations; listen; and give silent assent to spoken expressions. Here, too, liturgical form comes through the actions of responsive worshipers. They are not mere audience but highly involved participants in the unfolding activity and dialogue of worship. Their performance ends not at the dismissal: "Go in peace; serve the Lord." The performance of worshipers continues in the community and the world by their going forth to serve.[17] As Richard Lischer makes clear, "meaning is disclosed in the community's performance of the text in worship and in its witness in the world."[18]

What is less clear is that God is also active and performing in worship. Jana Childers recalls that it was Søren Kierkegaard who saw the similarities between worship and drama. As one who frequented theater and worship, he highlighted the parallels between them and "pictured the congregation as on stage as the actors playing to God in the audience—with the preacher prompting from the wings."[19] As helpful as it is for Childers's thesis that worship is theater, there is a blur in Kierkegaard's vision. It suggests that as audience, God attends worship but sits in the house as passive receptor of the unfolding drama. What is nearer the mark is that God is present but active alongside the few and the many who play out their roles. In a sense, there is no audience in worship. Even though worshipers usually sit in rows as do theater-goers and listen to the reading of the Word or the sermon, the "audience" is involved and given the opportunity to respond to what God is doing in the performance of the Word. Whether they are among the many who assemble or the few who lead, all people are active in worship as non-audience. And so is God.

God has a share in the activity of worship. Which share? The lion's share (to borrow an apt image from Twain). God not only performs *with* those who worship, but performs as the most active of those present. In baptism, it is not the presiding minister who baptizes. Nor is it a gift bestowed by the community. The presider enacts the command to baptize. The community responds to the promise of spiritual adoption and enfolds the initiated into the community. But it is God who performs the baptism, making water a sign of cleansing and renewal. In Holy Communion, the presider speaks of the promise of Jesus' presence in the meal but does not concoct the real presence of Christ. This, too, is God-given. What we do as presiders, preachers, and people who assemble in response to God's promises is to join in the divine self-disclosure that Charles Bartow speaks of. As agents of God's activity we participate in "God's self-performance."[20]

DIVINE PRESENCE AND PERFORMANCE

As suggested in the previous chapter, any ritual might be significant for participants simply as an artistic form that resonates with people according to its power to bear a resemblance to human experience. Yet ritual that does not presume the presence and activity of the Divine is spiritually vacant. It is not the ritual of worship. Nor is it something to put one's trust in.

There was no lack of trust in the prayer of Jesus, who prayed the intimate "Abba" as if the Creator were as near as breath and as caring as a parent. Likewise, those biblical figures who made petition directly to the historical Jesus did so with an expectation that Jesus would deliver according to their need. "Lord, teach us to pray" (Luke 11:1), implored the disciples; "I believe; help my unbelief" (Mark 9:24), pleaded the father of the possessed boy; "Only speak the word, and my servant will be healed" (Matt. 8:8), entreated the centurion. In each case, the address was made to a present Christ[21] who responded according to the faith placed in him. The real presence of God comes with the expectation of God's willingness to be mobilized according to the needs of God's people. It is this same mobilizing presence, though unseen, that we encounter in our assemblies.

Usually that presence is there to bring the gifts of God's grace. God never shows up in worship with empty hands. Like the favorite aunt who always arrives with a special gift, God brings good things to the people of faith. And we, like indulged children, come with hands open, expecting the bounty. Good news for the poor, release for the captives, sight to the blind, freedom for the oppressed, and the proclamation of God's favor are some of the gifts Isaiah speaks of (Isa. 61:1–2). When Jesus preached in his home synagogue, these are what he claimed to bring (Luke 4:16–21). When he preached on the mount, he promised blessings, even happiness (μακάριος) to the poor in spirit, those who mourn, the meek, those who thirst for righteousness, the merciful, the pure in heart, the peacemakers, and those persecuted for his sake (Matt. 5:2–11). God's presence in Christ also promises peace (John 14:27), forgiveness of sins (Luke 6:37), and eternal life (Matt. 25:34; John 14:2).

At other times God's presence in worship brings something else that is needed, although unwanted: judgment and correction. Even when God appears to be dissatisfied with a people, God still appears. At these times, God acts not like the favorite aunt, but like a loving, corrective parent. We see this in the Old Testament where, through the prophet Amos (chap. 5), God declares, "I hate, I despise your festivals, and I take no delight in your solemn assemblies." It is the presence of an angry God who refrains from looking upon their burnt offerings and accepting their grain offerings. "Take away from me," says the present One, "the noise of your songs. I will not listen to the melody of your harps." In the face of the people's displeasing conduct, God comes not with a blessing but with a promise of destruction and deportation. Likewise, in the New Testament we see that God's presence in worship has the potential to bring not what the people want but the correction that they need. Paul warns the Corinthians (1 Cor. 11:17–33) that those who eat the Lord's Supper in an unworthy manner receive not the Christ of forgiveness but the Christ of judgment. Whether bringing grace or correction, God is present and active when God's people gather.

But, though God is present and active in worship, there is something undeniably missing in our perception of that presence. As I suggested earlier, our knowledge of God's presence is not one that can be seen or verified in any empirical sense. It is a knowledge born of more sentient perceptions.

THE HIDDEN PRESENCE

Over a century ago, Henry Alford captured in his hymn one of the mysteries of our faith:

> We walk by faith and not by sight;
> With gracious words draw near;
> O Christ, who spoke as none e'er spoke;
> "My peace be with you here."
> We may not touch your hands and side,
> Nor follow where you trod;
> But in your promise we rejoice,
> And cry, "My Lord and God."[22]

Thomas needed to see in order to believe and only then could he cry, "My Lord and my God" (John 20:28). But we believe without seeing. Even though we proclaim and encounter the presence of God in worship, it is an unseen presence. Our faith is, as the writer to the Hebrews put it, "the assurance of things hoped for, the conviction of things not seen" (11:1).

There is a hidden quality about the God we worship,[23] an air of mystery that makes the presence seem removed. Indeed, along with the promise of God's presence in worship, there is also the promise of an absence that will be filled only at the time of the eschaton. The promise "Remember, I am with you always, to the end of the age" (Matt. 28:20) stands alongside the promise "I will come again and will take you to myself" (John 14:3). Presence and absence stand side by side in faith and in worship. As David Power has shown in *Unsearchable Riches: The Symbolic Nature of Liturgy*, the symbols of the liturgy help us to embrace both God's revelation and the negativity of God's absence. "The church celebrates," he says, "the presence of its Lord in these symbols, while at the same time recognizing the absence that will endure until the eschaton."[24]

Yet the absent quality of God implies not a lack of presence, but the presence of mystery. It is a mystery that calls forth a response and draws us into the liturgical dialogue with God. Our response to the mystery is to act *as if* the God who is unseen is nonetheless among us.

The sense of acting "as if" is a helpful way of understanding our response to a God who is both present and hidden. In other facets of life, it works like this. We act as if someone or something is present when we encounter a *sign*[25] of that presence. When we see the sign of a leaping deer alongside the road, we begin to drive more attentively, as if a deer were there to leap in front of us. When we see the morning's frost on the window, we dress for the day as if it were cold outside. When we hear someone call out a friend's name, we look around as if that friend were arriving. The signs are not themselves the objects of our interest. Our interests lie in the actual deer that might cause an accident, the cold that might make us uncomfortable, the friend who is coming to be with us. Yet the sign gives an indication of the presence of the object of our interest even when we have not yet seen or experienced that object.

In worship, we encounter *signs* of God's presence and they lead us to act *as if* God were there. Thus, Gordon Lathrop can say that when we surround the hearing of God's Word in worship with singing, "we sing to God as if God were present."[26] One might be tempted to say that we sing or pray to God in worship *because* God is present. When the centurion pleaded for his beloved servant as he stood in Jesus' presence, he addressed his appeal not as if Jesus were there, but directly to the one who stood before him. But the One whom we stand before is cloaked in mystery and veiled from sight. Therefore, Lathrop's "as if" is proper in that it suggests the hiddenness of God's presence and implies the force of the present/absent tension that is known by those who "walk by faith and not by sight."

One of the modes of God's hidden presence is as it occurs in the Body of Christ. We are, as Paul asserts, "the body of Christ and individually members of it" (1 Cor. 12:27). But we know who we are and how un-Christlike we can be. When we gather for worship, it is not in the likeness of Christ, but in the image of human sinfulness. We are more individuals of self-indulgence and self-gratification than individual members of a selfless and holy people. When Gardner C. Taylor once preached of the transformation that can come from knowing God, he suggested that the saintly appearance of those who loved the Lord might confuse the angels and when they looked from Jesus to the believer, they would ask, "Which one is Jesus?"[27] Such is our hope in the transforming power of God's Word that we can be, with Paul, imitators of Christ. But human behavior betrays the difference and no angel would long be fooled. Neither would God.

Yet, through baptism, we have put on Christ (Gal. 3:27)—or, because God is the active one in baptism, God has put Christ on us. When God looks at us in Christ, God sees us *as if* we were what God would have us be.[28] This implies that we should live *as if* all that God would have us be in Christ is true of us. God's perception of us as Christ is founded not in our actual experience of godly living but in God's redemptive action, which looses us from our own humanness and frees us to be part of the Body of Christ. We are *simil justis et peccator* and, thereby, one with Christ. The Christ in us individually and corporately, as in the Body of Christ, is veiled in the mystery of sanctification. When the Body of Christ assembles for worship, Christ is present in it, yet hidden by its all too human constituency. Thus, while Christ is unseen, the gathering itself becomes the sign of Christ's presence.

We have spoken of the ways in which worship is art and have seen how worship is suffused with the quality of virtual experience. In the gathering of the Body of Christ, we see that virtuality at work in us. In our better moments, as we have experienced forgiveness for our sins, we have been moved to Christly imitation. Not only does *God* act as if we were Christ, *we* act as if we were Christ and imitate his capacity for love. In her work on preaching as theater, Jana Childers refers to the great drama teacher Stanislavski. He spoke of an image called "The Magic If." "The word *if* is magic," Childers explains, ". . . because it gives us permission to be something other than what we are."[29] In faith, we know that we are not Christ, but we act *as if* we were Christ when we perfect our faith through loving action. Our action is a sign that Christ is in us. Acting as if we were Christ is not our entire experience of the life of faith, but it is one of its constituent elements. To assemble as the Body of Christ is to gather in semblance of the Christ who saves and transforms us. Worship as virtual experience encompasses our imitation of the Crucified One. The God who is present in all things generally is present in us specially as the Body of Christ, hidden in the gathering form of people who imitate Christ's love.

We encounter the present One without seeing, but not without tasting and touching, as when we eat and drink the bread and wine of Holy Communion. And we encounter the present One through hearing. Hearing God's presence occurs in two ways: through the reading of Scripture and the preaching of the Word.

The hidden One is known through Scripture. Personal presence is usually accompanied by the sound of a voice. When a voice is heard, it is a sign that its owner is near. When people spoke to the historical Jesus, they knew him not only by recognition of his appearance but by the distinctiveness of his voice. Even Saul, who, on the way to Damascus, fell to the ground in blindness, knew it was Jesus who addressed him as he listened to the voice that spoke from the vision. When God spoke out of the cloud at the moment of transfiguration, the voice disclosed the immediacy and immanence of the divine presence. There was no need to act as if in these circumstances. People acted because God was there, present with voice and substance. Saul fell to the ground in fear; Peter was so terrorized on the mountain that, in his confusion, he spoke in non sequitur.

Sheep recognize the voice of their shepherd, Jesus tells us (John 10:27), but the voice of our Shepherd comes to us today not firsthand as original speech. The voice of God comes to us secondhand, veiled in the words of Scripture that are read aloud in worship as a sign of God's hidden presence. As Peter Fink has observed, through readers proclaiming the Word, "the Christ who has gathered now speaks and reveals to the assembly the ways of God."[30] This has long been part of God's way of speaking and being present to us.

We first hear of the public reading of Scripture in worship in the book of 2 Kings. When the high priest Hilkiah found the book of the covenant in the temple, King Josiah called for a special temple service in which it could be read:

> Then the king directed that all the elders of Judah and Jerusalem should be gathered to him. The king went up to the house of the LORD, and with him went all the people of Judah, all the inhabitants of Jerusalem, the priests, the prophets, and all the people, both small and great; he read in their hearing all the words of the book of the covenant that had been found in the house of the LORD. (2 Kgs. 23:1–2)

During the time of the Babylonian captivity, as God's exiled people began to meet for worship in synagogues, the reading of Scripture became an integral part of their experience of connectivity to their faith and homeland. By New Testament times, the reading of Scripture constituted the principal part of public worship in the synagogue. It became common to invite a visiting rabbi to offer the readings and a commentary on them.[31] In one instance, Luke tells us, that visitor was Jesus. At the inauguration of his ministry he went "as was his custom" to worship in the synagogue in Nazareth, read from the prophet Isaiah, and claimed his place as the one of whom Isaiah spoke (Luke 4:16–22). Scriptural reading naturally became a part of the worship pattern for the early church. Justin describes the pattern in his *First Apology* written to the Roman emperor in the middle of the second century: "And on the day which is called the Sun's Day there is an assembly of all who live in the towns or the country and the memoirs of the Apostles or the writings of the prophets are read for as long as there is time" (*Apologia* I, 67).[32] A practice firmly established in the history of our faith, the Scriptures "continue to be read in church," says Geoffrey Wainwright, "and in and through their reading . . . the Lord makes himself present."[33]

When God's Word is read in worship today, we hear it *as if* it were an original word. We hear it as if it were the voice of God speaking from the mountain or from the burning bush. We respond to it as if it were the voice of the Shepherd calling his sheep. We surround it with singing as if we were in God's presence. We honor the reading of the Gospel by standing, as if Christ were physically present to speak to us firsthand. We do these things because we know that the words we hear are the Words God gives us and that they are a sign that God is with us, actively bringing the message of grace or reproval. When the Word is read in worship, it is a human voice we hear, but it is not ordinary human speech. It is, as Charles Bartow says, "God's human speech," which is "with us, about us, against us, and thereby for us."[34] When we hear the voice of this speech, it signifies that its Author is near.

There is another mode of God's human speech[35] and sign of God's hidden presence. Although we encounter the present One without seeing, it is not without hearing: it comes to us through the voice of the preacher.

The hidden One is known through preaching. Young children are sometimes easily confused as to matters of faith. Seeing their pastor sweep by in a long flowing robe, listening to him or her speak with authority, seeing the pastor command the attention, often admiration, of the congregation, a child frequently jumps to a very natural conclusion. "There goes Jesus," a little voice will say, and some amused adult will tell the pastor and suggest that the record needs to be set straight.

With that as the only exception, I should think, no one would ever mistake the preacher for Jesus. The preacher is not Jesus. Nor is the voice of the preacher the voice of Jesus. Even the words expressed in the sermon are not Jesus' words, except as quoted from Scripture. When God's Word is preached, Jesus Christ is not preaching.[36] But, by means of a human voice, Christ is being proclaimed and is present in the proclamation. In preaching, Christ is both hidden and present. Richard Lischer captures this present/absent tension by saying, "Insofar as preaching rearticulates the saving themes and offers the life of God in Christ, it is Jesus himself who is the preacher, blessing *our* sermons with his presence" [italics added].[37] As preachers, they are *our* sermons. But they are not our messages. We proclaim Christ and, through that proclamation, Christ is present. No one has put it more boldly or concretely than Dietrich Bonhoeffer:

> The proclaimed word is the incarnate Christ himself. As little as the Incarnation is the outward shape of God, just so little does the proclaimed word present the outward form of a reality; rather, it is the thing itself. The preached Christ is both the Historical One and the Present One. . . . the proclaimed word is the Christ himself walking through his congregation as the Word.[38]

Christ walking through the congregation is a vivid image: the flowing robe, the commanding voice, the people's rapt attention. No wonder the children are confused.

But we are not to be confused, nor are we to confuse those who listen to our preaching. Preaching needs to be transparent so as to disclose not our voice, nor our opinions, biases, passions, or peeves. It must disclose the hidden One so that Christ can meet and interact with those who listen to us as if we were he.

DISCLOSING THE HIDDEN PRESENCE

In worship, the hidden One is present and active with the few and the many. Making that presence known is one of the chief goals of worship leadership. Our task is to aid in what Bartow calls the "divine self-disclosure" by attending to it "with all the varied means appropriate to it."[39] The Gospel of John tells of some Greeks who once came to Philip and said, "Sir, we wish to see Jesus" (12:21). Those who had heard the story of Jesus were eager to meet him and experience firsthand the power of his transforming love. It is a pattern still repeated today. People come together to meet the God who made them, to be touched and enlightened by the Holy Spirit, to meet the Christ who saves them and gives them strength and hope. When the people of God assemble for worship, they gather as if to say to the preacher and ministers, "Friends, we wish to see Jesus." To serve as Philip to the people is the minister's role: to perform in ways that disclose the One whose presence is hidden. "Liturgy's duty," says Aidan Kavanagh, "is to enflesh and serve the *logos*, and true liturgy celebrates nothing but the active presence of the Three in One."[40] If this is liturgy's duty, then responsibility for the performance of that duty falls to those who plan, execute, and lead in public worship.

Making God's presence known to the assembly is a responsibility that relates to the way that people are drawn into worship's dialogical web. It occurs between the few who lead and the many who assemble as preachers and ministers express themselves in sermons and prayer and in the language of worship leadership. This expression takes the form of public discourse. But, as we saw in the first chapter, the language of worship needs to be nondiscursive as well if it is to speak to people of matters too deep for words. Discursive language can suffice for the literal expression of instruction and definition. But language that intends to disclose the divine presence and to enable God's Word to reach deeply is presentational language, selected according to the logical rightness and necessity of expression in order to yield sentient and revelatory results.

Christ is revealed when worshipers are drawn into the Word by preachers who know how to create a realm of virtual experience. In the sermon, real time is suspended as the listener enters into a world of human concern that is created by the preacher. Within this world walk both the seeker and the Sought. "I felt as if you were preaching directly to me," the listener often responds to the preacher. "I just wanted you to know that I am that person you spoke of today," the preacher hears. The preacher does not need to tell each particular parishioner's story for the sermon to connect with people. He or she merely creates a virtual world, one that is real enough for listeners to perceive a connection between their condition and the broader human condition. In this world walk the needs and concerns of people who seek refuge in Christ. There, too, walks Christ who is present in this virtual realm to bring peace, comfort, blessing, hope, and forgiveness. Or he is there to bring judgment and correction, if that is the need. But it is no virtual Christ that is disclosed, any more than it is the mere likeness of human need that is represented. It is real hunger met with the real Bread of Life, genuine thirst met with Living Water. Out of the realm of semblance steps the Christ who walks up and down the aisles, in and among the pews, out of the words of the sermon into the hearts of the people.

The disclosure of God's presence happens also in the language of prayer. Here, too, is a virtual realm in which matters of the heart are given the shape of lament, thanksgiving, petition, and praise. The prayer leader carefully crafts his or her language so as to draw the assembly into the activity of divine intercourse. Through clarity of focus, the speaker directs people's minds and hearts to the One whose presence is known but not seen. Concerns of the heart are spoken, people respond in silent or verbal assent, and the God who is addressed hears the need and prepares the divine response.

Some of the language used by worship leaders is less scripted than sermon and prayer. Instructions as to movement, flow, and intention are given as worship services proceed. Announcements and introductions often become important parts of an assembly's communal life. Whereas these messages do not carry the weight of Word and prayer, they are important words that require care if they are to direct people to see the One they came to meet. Too many words, or ill-chosen, clumsy expression can lead people not down the path where hiddenness is revealed but down backstreets of confusion and side alleys that direct people away from an encounter with worship's central figure. The request "We wish to see Jesus" is answered with diversion. That which is revealed is not God's presence but the speaker's lack of preparation, need for recognition, or concern for incidentals. The unspoken message is clear, and it is received as from a shifty salesperson: "Yes, I know you wish to see Jesus, but can I interest you in something else (like the fact that the mistakes in the bulletin are not mine, or that the choir has been working long and hard on the piece about to be rendered for your enjoyment, and so on)?" To put it more sardonically, we can paraphrase Groucho Marx, who once said, "I can see it all now, you standing in front of a hot stove; but I can't see the stove!" Worship leaders need to express themselves in such a way as to avoid the response, "I can see you, but I can't see Jesus."

CONCLUSION

Our purpose in this chapter has been to consider issues of presence and performance in worship. We have seen how the God who is generally present in the cosmos is present in greater degree and in varying ways in the Word and sacraments. Performance was explored as to the legitimacy of its place in worship. It is a natural part of all occurrent arts, including the arts of preaching, public prayer, and worship leadership. The category of performance extends to what God's people do when they enter into the liturgical dialogue of worship and what God does when grace and judgment are brought in company with God's presence. Our liturgical encounter with God occurs within the tension of divine presence and absence. Yet we have seen that the hidden God is known in the Body of Christ and revealed in God's Word as read and preached. Finally, we came to the proposition that chief among the desires of worshiping people is the wish to see Jesus. Disclosing the presence of the hidden God is the role of preachers and worship leaders. In part, this is accomplished when preachers and those who pray and lead in public worship craft their language with an awareness of their aesthetic responsibility.

In the concluding three chapters of this book, the practical aspects of aesthetic responsibility as they relate to preaching, crafting prayers, and speaking in worship will be considered in detail. But, before engaging in these matters of performance and practice, we will explore a third theological consideration, the performatory power of the words we use in our liturgical expression.

3

Only Say the Word

When he entered Capernaum, a centurion came to him, appealing to him and saying, "Lord, my servant is lying at home paralyzed, in terrible distress." And he said to him, "I will come and cure him." The centurion answered, "Lord, I am not worthy to have you come under my roof; but only speak the word, and my servant will be healed. For I also am a man under authority, with soldiers under me; and I say to one, 'Go,' and he goes, and to another, 'Come,' and he comes, and to my slave, 'Do this,' and the slave does it." When Jesus heard him, he was amazed and said to those who followed him, "Truly I tell you, in no one in Israel have I found such faith. . . ." And to the centurion Jesus said, "Go; let it be done for you according to your faith." And the servant was healed in that hour.

Matt. 8:5–13

Preachers and leaders of public worship use words to accomplish their roles. We have seen how figurative forms of speech are effective as means to reach spiritual and psychological depths and to transform the lives of those who worship. Because the presence of God is disclosed in the language of worship, we have also seen the importance for preachers and those who lead in prayer and other verbal liturgical forms to undertake their roles with aesthetic sensitivity. We have looked at issues of performance, both the performance of the hidden One in worship and the performance of those whose responsibility it is in worship to disclose by their leadership the divine presence. In this chapter, we will follow the line of the performance motif and demonstrate the performatory power of liturgical language. Here, too, the argument is toward the appropriation of aesthetic responsivity by those who serve as custodians of these powerful words.

43

Words have power. They express what is going on inside of us, give shape to our feelings, and provide structure for our thoughts. Once we learn how to speak, we even think in terms of language. We wonder what form our thoughts took when we were very young and had not learned to use words. We know that we had thoughts about hunger, pain, joy, love, and fear. But we cannot remember or imagine what those thoughts must have been like before we had words to give them shape. We did use certain sounds to give our thoughts and feelings expression. A cry registered pain, hunger, or fear. Laughter indicated joy, contentment, or love. Parents of young children struggle to understand the meaning of these nonverbal communications. When my newborn daughter suffered from colic, her constant crying made us distressingly aware that she had some form of discomfort. We could not, however, pinpoint its cause. Was it physical pain, as from stomach gas? Was it fear? Or was it her reaction to the bright, dry, loud world about her that was so different from the warm, dark, wet womb that had previously been her entire universe? Even her doctors could not tell us the cause of her discomfort because she could not give an accurate account of her feelings through words. In later years, it was a comfort to be able to ask, "Where does it hurt?" and treat her according to pain she could speak of. Words give us the power of self-expression.

The power of words goes beyond expressing what is going on inside of us. They also provide us with the potency of intercommunication. As words give shape to our thoughts and feelings they go out of us as speech and convey their form to others. "My voice really goes out of me," says Walter Ong. "But it calls not to something outside, but to the inwardness of another. It is a call of one interior through an exterior to another interior."[1] Thus, by using discursive language we can interchange elements of cognition with others. And through presentational language we can communicate matters of emotion and sentience that resonate in the interiors of others.

When our words leave us, they have the power to effect good or ill. In *What Language Shall I Borrow?* Brian Wren speaks of the power of language for ill effect. He uses the examples of Nazi propaganda and the language surrounding Atlantic slave trade and Native American derision to demonstrate the political and economic power of language.[2] These well-known examples illustrate how "Words can start people marching in the streets—and can stir others to start stoning the marchers."[3] H. H. Farmer also spoke of the power of words. In reflecting on the childhood chant "Sticks and stones may break my bones, but words will never hurt me," he said:

> Nothing could be more false. Words can and do hurt much more penetratingly and destructively than sticks and stones. Perhaps it was because deep down we knew that words can hurt us most frightfully that we were so anxious to protest that they did not.[4]

Words also have the power to effect good things. By now, people are familiar with the psychological principle known as the self-fulfilling prophecy. By the words we use, we have the power to shape the lives of those to whom we speak. The parent helps to create kind children by speaking of them as "good" and "polite." Teachers shape students through praise and positive reinforcement. And preachers mold their listeners into the body of Christ through the accumulative power of preaching. This is accomplished, says Richard Lischer, when preaching assumes the image of "pilgrimage" or "journey" such that *"preaching, as opposed to individual sermons, forms a community of faith over time."*[5]

The positive power of language can be found in another form. It occurs in language that performs as it is uttered. Such language is known by philologists as "performative" or "performatory" language.

THE POWER OF PERFORMATORY SPEECH

I once made the kind of mistake every pastor dreads. It occurred as I was performing a wedding for a couple whose names were Paul and Anne. Lurking in my memory was a speech pattern that momentarily supplanted the one I was to have spoken. More familiar to me than "Paul and Anne" was the pattern of the names of two friends, Paul and Linda. "Paul and Linda": these were names I frequently associated together in my personal life. "Let's have Paul and Linda over for dinner." "Paul and Linda called today." "I saw Paul and Linda at the market yesterday." The habit of my personal association of these two names stepped forward in the public moment of officiation and wrested control of my speech. I blurted out: "Do you Paul take *Linda* to be your wife?" Anne, slack-jawed, stared at me in painful disbelief. The wedding party gasped. Paul squirmed, but managed to mutter a correction. "It's Anne," he mumbled, and I read in his glaring look the rest of the message he was thinking ("It's Anne, stupid!").

"I take Anne to be my wife" is a powerful thing to say. It has a transforming effect on Paul's entire life. No longer single, no longer independent, but, by virtue of those words, he becomes one flesh with Anne, not with Linda. They are bound together in all of life's circumstances and in private and public ways. They are personally joined in love, morally responsible for the other's welfare, and legally united as a family. "Do you take Linda?" in this unhappy circumstance, has the power to create not union but distress. At another time and with another, happier Paul, the words "Do you take Linda?" did have the power to perform successfully the matrimonial function.

In the very act of saying the words "I take you Anne," the action is performed. Paul doesn't actually take Anne in any binding personal, moral, or legal sense until he *says* that he does. The power of these words is in their utterance.

They perform precisely as they are spoken. Beginning with the moment of Paul's proclamation and lasting from that moment forward, Anne is Paul's wife. And, in her "I take you Paul" is enacted the reciprocal action by which he is bound to her.

Philosopher J. L. Austin has spoken of these operative kinds of utterances as "performative" or "performatory." In *How to Do Things with Words*, he examines the forms of locution that perform the subject of their intent in the act of their being spoken. Although Austin coined both terms, he prefers "performative" to "performatory" because it is "shorter, less ugly, more tractable, and more traditional in form."[6] However, in recent years the term "performative" has been widely used in performance theory as relating to matters of artistic execution. For example, Ronald Pelias, author of *Performance Studies: The Interpretation of Aesthetic Texts*, uses "performativity" to refer to performance situations that are transactional dialogues between speakers and listeners involving aesthetic texts.[7] Therefore, Austin's term of second choice, "performatory," becomes more manageable here for our discussion of the power of liturgical words. Free from connotations of artistic performance, "performatory" issues can be seen as over against "performative" concerns. As we shall see, given the power of performatory forms of expression, there is a theological imperative at work for people who preach and lead in public worship. The theological principle derives from biblical imagery surrounding acts of divine utterance and relates performative (having to do with artistic execution) considerations to the performatory power of liturgical language.

Austin gives several examples of performatory utterances:

> "I do (. . .take this woman to be my lawful wedded wife)"—as uttered in the course of the marriage ceremony.
> "I name this ship the Queen Elizabeth"—as uttered when smashing the bottle against the stem.
> "I give and bequeath my watch to my brother"—as occurring in a will.
> "I bet you sixpence it will rain tomorrow."[8]

In these examples, it is clear that the speaker is not describing an action about to be undertaken. The speaker is actually doing that which is being spoken of. To say "I do" is to accomplish the marriage. To say "I name this ship" is to give the name in that moment. To say "I bet you sixpence" is to join into a contract and the wager commences as the words are spoken. Another example is the use of the word "promise." To say "I promise you" is to bind the speaker to another person or group in an expectation of fulfillment. The relationship of obligation and expectation is set as the words are uttered.

There are, of course, circumstances that would render such statements false or nonperformatory. These are, as Austin calls them, unhappy or infelicitous circumstances.[9] Infelicities occur when certain conditions are not met. For example, the particular circumstances and persons must be appropriate to the event for it to be accomplished. Thus, when the words "I take you Paul" and "I take you Anne" are spoken during the wedding rehearsal, no marriage is performed because it is the wrong circumstance. And, when the words "Do you, Paul, take Linda?" are said to Paul and Anne, speaking the wrong person's name does not oblige Paul in any way to any Linda.

Some performatory statements are *explicit* in that they state plainly the action that is achieved in their utterance. For example, "I hereby claim" indicates unambiguously that the speaker is making a claim and that it is happening as it is stated. Other performatory statements are *implicit*, or *inexplicit*. In them is implied the power of enactment, though not so specifically stated. "Go!" implies the force of "I order you to go!"[10]

As he explores the issues of language and its force, Austin also uses the terms *locution, illocution, perlocution.* By *locution,* he refers to any general statement of description or fact. *Illocutionary* utterances have performatory force in that they perform an action in their being spoken. *Perlocutionary* utterances are those which have the power to produce certain consequential effects on the listener. If we follow Austin's program to its completion, we find that he concludes that all locutionary statements contain performatory force and that all illocutionary statements are locutionary.[11] In other words, he determines that the distinctions become blurred between statements that are locutionary and illocutionary when one considers the fullness of meaning as given by mood, circumstance, and intent. For our purposes, however, we shall take advantage of the distinction that Austin draws between ordinary statements and those that perform an action and, thus, have performatory force or power.[12]

The power of these utterances to accomplish things derives, in part, from presumptions that are understood by speaker and audience. The successful use of the words "I do," for example, presumes the setting of a marriage ceremony, the possession of a valid marriage license, and the agreement of bride and groom. Austin speaks of two types of presumptions. The first is *implication*: "My saying 'the cat is on the mat' implies that I believe it is. . . .We cannot say, 'the cat is on the mat but I do not believe it is.'"[13] The second type of presumption is called *presupposition*: "'All Jack's children are bald' presupposes that Jack has children. We cannot say 'All Jack's children are bald but Jack has no children,' or 'Jack has no children and all his children are bald.'"[14] The realization that performatory utterances are imbedded with implication and presupposition is especially helpful as we consider two ways that they function in worship. The first has to do with the implied source of power at work in liturgical language. The second deals with language that is inexplicitly performatory because it presupposes the presence of an activity that is not explicitly stated.

There is both human and divine power implied in the use of performatory liturgical language. For people who preach and lead in public prayer and worship, Austin's category of performatory utterance is instructive. Through it we learn of the distinctive power of the words we use. In some of this language, the implication is that the force of the speaker's intent and capacity to fulfill it are at work. To say "I promise" effects an obligation that relies on the speaker's power to fulfill it. Likewise, for a worship leader to speak the words "I welcome you into the Body of Christ" to the newly baptized is to presume upon the ability of that person to offer and extend genuine welcome. In other circumstances, the implied source of power to bring fulfillment to the minister's words is divine. Though it is we who speak in liturgy, word, and prayer, some of the things we say are spoken in God's behalf. In these we rely on God's presence and performance to bring them to completion. Consider this example: "I declare to you the forgiveness of your sins." Here we have both forces at work simultaneously. When the celebrant says, "I declare," it is with his or her own power that the declaration is given. At the same time, the statement presupposes divine power to enact God's forgiveness as it is pronounced.

There is explicit and inexplicit performatory language in worship. Performatory language that is explicit states both the action being performed and the subject performing it. For example, to say "We pray" is to identify what is being done and who is doing it. The minister speaks the words, but the "we" indicates that the assembly is engaged in the act of prayer as the leader speaks the words in the congregation's behalf. Likewise, to say "The Lord bless you" indicates both the enactment of blessing and the divine force from which it derives. Here, as the presider speaks, it is God who performs the blessing. Other liturgical statements are what we might call *inexplicit.* Although they manifest no explicit performatory character, they have performatory power in that they presume God's presence and activity and they enact powerful events as they are spoken. The words "Your sins are forgiven," in both Scripture and liturgy, have performatory power to enact forgiveness as they are stated. Saying "The peace of Christ be with you" presumes upon God's love in Christ to fulfill the grant of peace.

Our next step will be to explore the place and power of performatory utterances in worship. Consideration of how preachers and worship leaders are the custodians of explicit and inexplicit performatory language points us toward the need for using words carefully and with artistic sensitivity. The performatory power of the words we speak in worship stems from what God has accomplished through the Word in creation.

LET THERE BE LIGHT

The original performatory word is that which is given inexplicitly in the first chapter of Genesis. By virtue of God speaking, the writer tells us, all things were accomplished. "Let there be light," God said, "and there was light" (1:3). Likewise, God said let there be a dome in the sky and lights in the dome to separate the day and the night and waters and creatures and vegetation, and finally, humankind. As each command was spoken, each was accomplished. God's Word came forth not to describe events that were going to occur or that had already taken place. The very act of God's speaking[15] was the accomplishment of God's intention. God's words were powerfully performatory. All things came into being at the command "Let there be."

It is impossible to miss the connection between the first chapter of Genesis and the first chapter of the Gospel of John. Here, too, the writer draws on the image of Word and demonstrates the power of what God has to say:

> In the beginning was the Word, and the Word was with God, and the Word was God. He was in the beginning with God. All things came into being through him, and without him not one thing came into being. What has come into being was life, and the life was the light of all people. (1:1–4)

In these words the performatory power of God's Word shines through. God speaks, or lets forth God's Word; all things spring into being, and life is generated. No human endeavor has been able to rearticulate what God does merely by speaking. Our procreative forces emerge from God's creative Word ("Be fruitful and multiply," Gen. 1:28). Our technological advances proceed out of the stuff that was first formed and given physical properties by divine utterance. Even our most technologically and genetically creative accomplishment, the process of cloning, does not presume for itself the power of the creation of life. The life of a cloned sheep derives not from human hands, but from the genetic material that is the key to all life. The holder of that key is God, and the hand that turns it belongs to the Word who was with God and who is God. The key turns only when the Word speaks and, in its performatory power, the miracle and mystery of life are made.

The performatory power of God's Word rings out in other places in Scripture. "I will make my covenant between me and you" (Gen. 17:2), God said to Abram and in so saying, established the promise of a nation of descendants and a new land. For Jacob, the Word was spoken by God's messenger. The stranger that wrestled with Jacob blessed him; in that blessing was transferred the covenant promise of a nation that was to be known by Israel, the name of Jacob's transformation (Gen. 32:22–32). For Hannah, the Word came from the priest Eli: "Go in peace," he said, "the God of Israel grant the petition you have made to him" (1 Sam. 1:18). In the words of Eli's prophetic pronouncement came the accomplishment of that for which Hannah had prayed: the opening of her womb. In the Gospel of Luke, Zechariah received a double portion of God's performatory power as given him in the message of the angel Gabriel. "Your wife Elizabeth will bear you a son" (1:13), said the angel and, with that, her womb was opened. But, because of his disbelief, the angel punished Zechariah. At the words "you will become mute" (1:20), Zechariah was rendered speechless and remained so until the birth of John. Likewise, Mary was given the news of birth and in the angel's message was the power of God's fulfillment. "The Holy Spirit will come upon you, and the power of the Most High will overshadow you" (1:35), the angel said; with the pronouncement came the accomplishment of God's intention.

The power of God's performatory Word was also released when the Word became flesh to dwell among us. "Be made clean," Jesus said to the leper, and "immediately his leprosy was cleansed" (Matt. 8:3). To the centurion he said, "Let it be done for you according to your faith" (8:13); with those words, the man's servant was healed. "Talitha cum" (Mark 5:41–42), Jesus said; instantly the little girl rose from her deathly sleep. And, to people throughout the Gospels he said, "Your sins are forgiven"; with his utterance came the moment of God's grace.

These scriptural stories report utterances that have performatory power only because they have the potency of divine speech. A person might say, "Let there be light" but could only accomplish his or her intention by completing it with a corresponding action, such as flipping the light switch or lighting a candle. For a person to say, "Little girl, arise" is to utter not a performatory statement, but a command that is accompanied by the expectation of a volitional action on the part of the object. But, when Jesus speaks it to a girl who has died, it has performatory power because it accomplishes Jesus' intention for her without a corresponding action or the girl's volition. When Jesus speaks these words or when people speak them in Jesus' name, the words do not describe an action but achieve it. Thus, when Peter spoke to Sapphira of the reason for her husband's death and of her accessory guilt, at the words "The feet of those who have buried your husband are at the door, and they will carry you out" (Acts 5:1–11), she, too, fell dead. Peter's words performed God's judgment in the act of their being spoken. Somehow the centurion sensed the performatory power of Jesus' words. "Only say the word," he said to Jesus, "and my servant will be healed."

PERFORMATORY WORDS IN WORSHIP

Certain words used by the assembly have inexplicit performatory power. "Amen," we say or sing as a response to prayer or to something we have heard. When we use the word it has the power to accomplish its meaning. The word means "So be it" or "I agree with the assertion." To say "amen" as a response in worship is not to describe one's form of agreement or to state that you are agreeing. It is not merely to express agreement but to enact it. There is a difference in the power of utterance between saying, "I find myself agreeing with your statement," and the spontaneous eruption of "Amen!" The former is a description; the latter has the performatory power of giving spiritual assent in the act of its vocalization. It has the same immediate power as does the phrase "I do" when it is uttered in a wedding ceremony.

The word "hosanna" is another liturgical word with performatory power. It is the shout of adoration spoken in the Gospels to Jesus as he rode on the colt into Jerusalem. When spoken by the crowd it not only indicated but also bestowed their praise. They shouted it not to say "We feel adoration," or "We announce our admiration." They shouted it to indulge in adoration. As it is used in the liturgy, the word has the same power: "Hosanna in the highest," we say or sing, indulging in an attitude of praise for the One who came and who is present still.

"Hallelujah" (or "alleluia") falls into the same performatory category. As an interjection, it has no synonym. Like the exclamation "Oh!" it reports nothing and is neither true nor false. It is simply an eruption of respect, awe, affection, and delight. It has to do with praise, but to shout "Praise!" sounds like a command. To shout or to sing "hallelujah" is not to command or to announce praise; it is to give praise, to burst forth in it.[16] Choral singers know the power of indulging in elegant explosions of musical praise. One thinks of the majestic "Hallelujah Chorus" in Handel's *Messiah*, the magnificence of which has always driven audiences to their feet; or the ethereal, undulating praise of Randall Thompson's "Alleluia." To sing this praise well is to be transported from carnal and temporal realms to a place of vision from which one perceives a glimpse of what heaven's praise must be. F. Melius Christiansen is reported to have said to his St. Olaf College choirs that when they sing an earthly "hallelujah," they join for a moment in the unending celestial "hallelujah" that is the perpetual praise of angels.

The language of public prayer contains performatory words. Consider the verbs of petition: to pray, to ask, to plead, to beg, to entreat, to implore, to beseech. To use these words in prayer is to explicitly engage in the action of their meaning. The words "We pray, O God . . ." are not spoken as a way of notifying God of our action or intention. To say "We pray" *is* to pray; to say "We beseech thee" *is* to beseech. To utter each of these verbs in public worship is to draw the hearts of the assembly together and to bid God's response to their concerns.

These words of petition are doubly powerful. First, they have the power of bringing to action the sentient yearnings of God's people. Deep are the needs when persons are driven to pray, beg, plead, and implore. If we beg for trivialities, our priorities are skewed and our request is soured by hyperbole at the least, and possibly even dishonesty. "I need some ice cream; I beg you," a child might say. But, here, there is no real need and the petition is merely an exaggerated expression of a desire. Petition in prayer relates to genuine human needs and expresses them with the fervor and vitality that are appropriate to heartfelt concerns. As prayers for peace, healing, wisdom, guidance, inspiration, patience, and forgiveness are uttered by the leaders of public prayer, they are given assent by the assembly. When the leader says "We pray" or "We implore you, Gracious God," it is with the power of enacting the assembly's prayer for things that are of central concern to their lives of faith and, sometimes, simply too deep for words.

Second, the words of petition are powerful because of the One to whom they are addressed and because of our expectation that they will be effectively answered. The strength we rely on in prayer comes from the power that effected all creation. Our petitions call on God to bring the same power to bear on our circumstances to inject life, inspiration, and interceding grace into the midst of our human needs.

Prayer also takes the form of praise and thanksgiving. Here again, operative words are at work. The word "praise" functions grammatically as a noun and a verb. It has no interjectory power and, as we have seen, shouting "Praise!" cannot mean the same thing as shouting "Hallelujah!" As a noun, the word merely describes a statement of or an attitude of esteem, admiration, or glorification. But, as a verb the word takes on explicit performatory power because it bestows the content of its esteem as it is spoken. To say "I praise you for the work you have done" is to give a person praise. To lead a congregation in prayer by saying "We praise you, O God, for your saving Word" is to draw the assembly together in a unified indulgence of praise. Likewise, we give thanks by saying so. Just as saying "thank you" to a person is to offer one's gratitude, leading a congregation to "thank God for the bounties of the harvest" is to bestow their appreciation in the act of the utterance.

Other words used in prayer leadership can have performatory power. "We pledge, O God, our commitment" offers a promise in behalf of a congregation that binds the members in a covenant with God. To speak the words "We repent" is to lead the assembly in the act of naming and turning from sin.

There is performative power in the liturgical words of the pastoral office. Some statements are usually reserved to be spoken by the pastor or priest. In *The United Methodist Hymnal* such statements are indicated by rubrics that authorize pastoral invocation: for example, "The pastor gives thanks appropriate to the occasion,"[17] or "The pastor makes the following statement to the congregation."[18] *The Lutheran Book of Worship* designates these pastoral pronouncements with a "P" for presiding minister, in contrast to "A" for assisting minister. In *The Hymnal 1982* of the Episcopal Church and in *Today's Missal* from Oregon Catholic Press, the rubrics indicate "Deacon" or "Cantor" for words to be spoken by laypersons while "Celebrant" designates statements reserved for pastoral execution. Even more than in the language of intercessory prayer, these pastoral pronouncements presuppose the presence and activity of God.[19] "The Lord bless you and keep you" is an example. When the presiding minister pronounces God's blessing upon God's people, it has performatory power. It is not the pastor's power that is being placed in action, but God's. Contrast this pronouncement with that given by the pastor or priest in a civil wedding. Pastoral power is rendered in the words "I now pronounce you husband and wife." But this power is established by the state and is given to the pastor by virtue of her or his training and ordination. In saying, however, "The Lord bless you," the presider calls on God's power to sanctify, support, and save God's people. The assembly trusts in God's presence and performance to execute the blessing as it is given.

I have suggested above that the pastoral pronouncement of forgiveness has the same spiritual force. The pastor may say in a personal statement, "Your sins are forgiven," to someone who has offended him or her in some way. In this instance, the statement has the power of offering to the offender the pastor's personal forgiveness for the offense. Forgiveness is rendered as the words are uttered, and it is a performatory statement. But, when the pastor serves in a public role to pronounce forgiveness for offenses against God, it is not personal forgiveness that is called into force but God's forgiveness. Thus, it is with divine authority that the pastor says in these or similar words:

> Almighty God, in mercy, has given Jesus Christ to die for us and for his sake forgives us all our sins. As a called and ordained minister of the Church and by Christ's authority, I therefore declare to you the entire forgiveness of all your sins.[20]

When these words are spoken, they presume upon the power of Christ who once spoke them himself. "Son, your sins are forgiven" (Mark 2:5), Jesus said to the paralytic whom he had healed, and his pronouncement had the power to effect and bestow his grace. Similarly, when the pastor or priest pronounces forgiveness in Jesus' name, the gift of grace comes with the pronouncement; it is a performatory statement with God's power behind it.

Pastors and priests are also custodians of God's performatory power in baptism and Holy Communion. When the presider says, "You are baptized in the name of the Father, and the Son, and the Holy Spirit," it is not an announcement but an enactment. The power to make bath become initiation does not rest in the hands of the celebrant; it comes from the Spirit of God. As it states in the 1982 World Council of Churches ecumenical statement, *Baptism, Eucharist, and Ministry*, "God bestows upon all baptized persons the anointing and promise of the Holy Spirit, marks them with a seal and implants in their hearts the first installment of their inheritance as sons and daughters of God."[21] Likewise, when worshipers hear the words "This is my body. . . . [T]his is the blood of the new covenant," the words and action of the presider are enacted before the table and within the gathering to disclose the presence of Christ. Christ comes not through any power that resides in the presider's hands but through God's promise that Christ is attendant in the assembly as the promise is spoken. The promise is given in the *verba* and enacted through the power of the Holy Spirit. Again, the pattern of God's performance is given in the ecumenical statement:

> The presence of Christ is clearly the centre of the eucharist, and the promise contained in the words of institution is therefore fundamental to the celebration. Yet it is the Father who is the primary origin and final fulfillment of the eucharistic event. The incarnate Son of God by and in whom it is accomplished is its centre. The Holy Spirit is the immeasurable strength of love which makes it possible and continues to make it effective.[22]

It will be remembered from chapter 2 that God's presence in worship comes in varying degrees and in special ways. The words of presidential leadership in the services of baptism and Holy Communion are performatory words in that God chooses to be present in special degree when they are uttered *in connection with* the assembly of God's people. To be clear about the theological implication here, let it be said that the celebrant's words are not construed to be confectory words. Such a misunderstanding led the young priest Martin Luther to tremble at the moment when he consecrated his first Mass. Luther assumed, as he had been taught, the priestly power of sacrificial reenactment. Thus, when he spoke the words "This is my body" and "This is the new testament of my blood," Luther nearly dropped the bread and wine and was tempted to run away from the altar.[23] In later years, he understood the use of those words more clearly and could relate their power to that of God's Word in creation. "Before the world existed, God said, 'Let there be a world,' and the world was. So he says here [in the Lord's Supper], 'Let this be my body,' and it is. . . ."[24] The words of sacramental celebration have the power of invoking God's presence through the Holy Spirit (epiclesis), but it comes not through particular formulas of speech. (For young Luther, the power resided uniquely in the priest's authority to utter the words *hoc est corpus meum* and *hoc poculum est novum testamentum*.) The words spoken by celebrants in baptism and Holy Communion have power as they are at work in the assembly of believers. The coming of God's Spirit in the sacraments cannot be tied to the moment of any particular human utterance but to the gathering of God's people. It is in the assembly that God promises to be present. The presider's words presume upon the power of that presence in the gathering to bring God's gifts of forgiveness and correction.

There is performatory power in preaching. Finally, as we consider the language of preaching, we rely here, too, on the presupposition that God is present and active as the preacher's words are delivered. Here, the performatory quality is strictly inexplicit, for the language of preaching involves more than explicit operative utterances (such as "I pray," "We implore you," and "God grant you peace"). The preacher's words are performatory in two ways.

We are pointed toward the first by Richard Lischer, who speaks of the category of "promise" as being the prototypical model for all preaching. "What is it that emerges from the grace of God, and what is the language we now seek to express? It is the promise."[25] Promise serves as an appropriate model for preaching because promise indicates "God's true preference for the kind of discourse he wishes to perpetuate with the church."[26]

Further, Lischer says:

> In the discussion of "promise" as a rhetorical form we maintain a balance between the absolute priority of God as the source, content, and life of all sermons, and an appreciation of the rhetorical shape in which that life is transmitted to us.[27]

In this model are strong, even Barthian presuppositions. Karl Barth also presumed the presence and activity of God in preaching as its source, content, and life. "Two things call for emphasis," Barth says. "First, God is the one who works [in preaching], and second, we humans must try to point to what is said in scripture. There is no third thing."[28] We see the parallel between Lischer and Barth made clearer as Barth explicates this statement. God is the source of preaching:

> Precisely because the point of the event of preaching is God's own speaking *(Deus loquitor)*, there can be no question of our doing the revealing in any way. . . . All the action that takes place in preaching, which lies between the first advent and the second, is the action of the divine Subject.[29]

God is the content of preaching:

> Preachers are under a restraint . . . that strips them of their own pro-
> gram. . . . A statement will be made. But in the strictest sense it will be
> God's statement. In preaching God himself presents what he wills to
> present, and will present. If preachers think they should present a
> theme of their own, it will anticipate what God himself wants to say.[30]

And God is the life of preaching:

> Preaching undoubtedly takes place within a human action, but this is
> an action which God has commanded and blessed, i.e., to which he has
> given a promise. . . . A human being becomes a hearer of the Word of
> God: This is our sanctification. The human being, the preacher, the
> listener—they are not left to themselves. They still are what they were
> before. But they are not left in peace. As what they are, they are placed
> in a *totally* new situation. Anything that we might say here about the
> power of God's Word to create anew is much too weak in view of the
> rest and unrest that are present when in faith a human being may grasp
> the calling of Jesus Christ. This is God's turning to us. How, then,
> should not all things be new?[31]

If promise is the prototypical model for preaching, as Lischer suggests and
Barth seems to support, then it has performatory power.[32] To say "I promise"
is to bind the speaker in an obligation of fulfillment. In the act of speaking the
promise, an expectation is created and the listeners wait for the moment of
completion. Likewise, when sermons declare God's promises as given in the
Scriptures they call upon God in the obligation of fulfillment of those
promises. As the words of the sermon are expressed, an expectation is created
that draws auditors into the anticipation that God is as good as God's Word.
Preaching is both claiming and proclaiming: A promise is made; we grasp it
and lay *claim* to God's obligation to fulfill it for us. And we *proclaim* that same
promise and fulfillment for others expecting that God will fulfill it through us.

Although it is we who speak in preaching, our words do not create the
expectation of our own power to fulfill the promise. We presume upon the
power of the Spirit to make good the words we proclaim as God's Word and
promise. Our words bear the message of hope as we nourish the expectation
that God's obligation and fulfillment are being enacted *pro nobis*, for us. The
words that we use when we craft our sermons are not explicitly performatory.
But, because they presuppose God's promise and imply its fulfillment, they
have the strong performatory force of words in which God's power inheres.

The second mode of preaching's performatory power is implied in its perlocutionary force (the power of words to produce consequential effects on the
listener). When God's Word is spoken as promise in preaching, the sermon
draws on the elements of that promise which accompany the divine presence.

In the second chapter, it will be remembered, the gifts of God's presence were said to include good news for the poor, release for the captives, sight to the blind, freedom for the oppressed, proclamation of God's favor, peace, forgiveness of sins, and eternal life. When necessary, they also include judgment and correction. Pronouncing these elements of presence and promise creates the anticipation that something will change.

Change occurs because the preacher's words have the power to transform. They are words that not only proclaim the promise and create the expectation of its fulfillment; they also have the potency to *bring* the promise to fulfillment. To speak of Christ's love is to let loose that loving Christ. He steps out of the words of the sermon and walks, as we have said, down the aisle and among the people. To proclaim release to those who are bound or healing to those who are ill is to release the powers of God's emancipation and restoration among those who need them. To speak among God's people of repentance is to bring the specter of God's judgment to those who need atonement. To speak of God's forgiveness is to let the power of God's grace loose among those who repent. "John the Baptist cried in the wilderness saying, 'Prepare ye the way of the Lord,'" reports Barbara Brown Taylor in one of her sermons, "and the way was prepared, his very words paving the desert where Jesus would walk."[33] When the preacher brings God's Word and promise to the people and when it is a Word that, as Barth says, God needs to speak to them, then it is a forceful and performatory word that is spoken.

The performatory power of the preacher's words has been vividly depicted by Barbara Brown Taylor. In the sermon quoted above, she was addressing a group of pastors and encouraging their careful use of the words that God gives them to speak. Here again, she says:

> You don't need a grand pulpit to utter [God's Words] from. Any old housetop will do. Take the sun room at the nursing home where you stand by the piano surrounded by wheelchairs full of old people, some of them dozing, some of them whimpering to go back to their rooms, less than half of them even aware that you are there. Say "resurrection" in their presence. Say "life everlasting." Say "remember." Just let those words loose in the room, just utter them in the light and trust them to do their work. Or speak to a support group for people with AIDS. Worship with them if you can, lay hands on their hands and pray for their healing. Say "mercy" to them. Say "comfort." Say "beloved children of God." Just let those words loose in the room. Just utter them and trust in their power to make people whole. Or let something you care about lead you to the steps of city hall where you stand staring into television cameras wondering what in the world you have gotten yourself into. Say "justice." Say "peace." Say "the righteousness of God," and never mind what other people say. Never mind that they walk past you without reading your sign or put you in the

back of a paddy wagon and take you away. God is in charge of the
result.34

Here is a potent image for preachers who understand that God is at work in
the sermon bringing power to the words they use to point to what is being
said in Scripture. Just let those words loose and trust in their effectiveness to
accomplish God's promise among God's people. Only say the word.

CONCLUSION

In this chapter we have been concerned with the power of words and the ways
that our liturgical language has been especially empowered by the God who
works in it. We have learned from J. L. Austin the power of illocutionary language and have drawn from his thesis the conviction that the language of worship has performatory power. Some words have the force of human intent
behind them. We find this in liturgical exclamations such as "amen,"
"hosanna," and "hallelujah." We find it also in the language of prayer, as in
"We pray, O God," "We beseech thee," "We praise you, O Christ," and "We
thank you, Good Lord." Other words glow with internal power because they
are pronouncements of God's performance: "The Lord bless you," and "I baptize you." Finally, we looked at the language of preaching and discovered how
the words we speak in sermons are performatory in two ways: as the pronouncement of God's promise and as language that has the perlocutionary
effect of achieving transformation in the lives of listeners.

What we have been talking about is the power inherent in the primary symbols of our art, words. If our words as preachers and leaders of worship and
prayer have such power, then these words need to be handled with care. We
need to learn to use these powerful words well if sermons, prayers, and liturgical language are to address us at the soul-deep level of faith, draw us into solidarity with other believers, and aid us in expressing things that are too deep
for words. We must seek skillfully to craft our language if it is to be the window through which Christ is revealed and the door through which he enters
to walk among his people. We are the custodians of the powerful words of
promise. To speak them well and handle them with care means that we attend
to matters of execution, performance, and artistic sensitivity. In other words,
we must assume the aesthetic responsibility associated with our roles as worship leaders.

In what manner shall we care for these words? Should they be handled as
if they were a loaded gun or a vial of Ebola virus? Barbara Brown Taylor says
we should treat them with the same care and respect that we would a stick of

dynamite.[35] We are reminded again of the fear of the young Luther who spoke the consecratory words of his first Mass. But, as Luther later learned, the words we use in worship and preaching should be handled with pastoral care and not necessarily with fear of endangerment. For one who has lived many years in the beautiful Sonoma Valley wine country, a more savory image springs to mind. Our ministerial words can be handled carefully as one carries a crystal goblet of fine wine. The words we use are the vehicle for God's presence and performance just as the crystal is the conveyance for the wine. When light catches on the cuts and facets of the crystal, it reflects and refracts; it moves in vivid patterns and reveals multiple levels of tone and intensity. The goblet is not the wine, but its clarity and beauty disclose the treasure within. Our purpose as preachers and worship leaders is to disclose the treasure, using language that has the most clarity and capacity to let its brilliance penetrate.

Before looking at the specific categories of sermon, prayer, and general liturgical language to see to matters of aesthetic selection and execution, I will attempt to bring focus to the material of the foregoing chapters by drawing the three threads of this theological cord together. We have said, first, that worship is art that creates the sense of virtual experience and relies on presentational symbols to address issues that are too deep for words. Second, we have explored God's presence and performance in worship and emphasized the role of preachers and worship leaders in disclosing God's presence. Finally, we have considered the performatory power that inheres in our liturgical expression. Because these issues of poetry, performance, and enactment have to do with aesthetic matters, we turn now to reflect on a theological imperative that compels preachers and worship leaders to perform their roles with excellence.

4

The Hiddenness of Excellence

Beware of practicing your piety before others in order to be seen by them; for then you have no reward from your Father in heaven. So whenever you give alms, do not sound a trumpet before you, as the hypocrites do in the synagogues and in the streets, so that they may be praised by others. Truly I tell you, they have received their reward. But when you give alms, do not let your left hand know what your right hand is doing, so that your alms may be done in secret; and your Father who sees in secret will reward you. And whenever you pray, do not be like the hypocrites; for they love to stand and pray in the synagogues and at the street corners, so that they may be seen by others. Truly I tell you, they have received their reward. But whenever you pray, go into your room and shut the door and pray to your Father who is in secret; and your Father who sees in secret will reward you.

Matt. 6:1–6

We have been speaking of artistic symbols and performance. Let me tell describe two scenes in which symbol and performance were at work.

The chapel at Duke University is a monumental Gothic structure which, though merely seventy years old, has been built with the grandeur of medieval European cathedrals. It is filled with beautiful carvings and statuary and features seventy-seven stained-glass windows depicting over eight hundred biblical characters and saints. As my family worshiped there one Sunday morning we were four among many: fifteen hundred strong were the voices that sang the opening hymn. The singing was accompanied by two magnificent pipe organs, one in the loft behind the worshipers, another in the choir at the front of the church. The hymns were also accompanied by a one-hundred-fifty-voice choir and a wind ensemble of twenty pieces. The sermon that morning was riveting;

the choral performances were numerous, intricate, and exquisite; the procession and recession were festive and accomplished with precision. Never ostentatious, but well planned and carefully executed, the service of worship was transporting. It was a moment out of time, a suspension of ordinary experience; a successful illusion. It was virtual experience in which the presentational symbols of architecture, visual art, Scripture, sermon, music, and movement worked together to create an hour of worship in which worshipers were drawn together and led to see Jesus. Never seen precisely, his presence was known as he walked among us in sermon and song.

In the village of Petra on the island of Majorca, there is a large, plain church. Hundreds of years old, it is the church in which Father Junipero Serra, the Spanish priest who founded many of the California missions, worshiped as a boy. It is still being used today. Each year, on the evening of January 5, the entire village gathers inside the church to celebrate the festival of Epiphany. The village priest begins the ceremony but does not play a large part in it. Some boys from the town are made up as Wise Men from the East and hold central place for a few moments. But the centerpiece of the ritual that unfolds in this service is the performance of a lad of seven years. Dressed in biblical garb, he assumes the role of priest and prophet. The boy has prepared an address for the people, a speech that is scripted and presented identically each year.

A few years ago, I was invited into this setting. The village had gathered in the cold, dimly lit church. There were men and women of every age; children of all sizes. Not a soul from the village would miss this night. Later on, in the brightly lit village square, the Wise Men would hand out gifts to every child of the town. But first, they gather for worship. I watched and listened carefully that evening as the boy-priest began to speak. Standing alone in the chancel, he addressed the thousand who had gathered. Speaking without aid of microphone, notes, or the prompting of the priest, he entered into an oration on the mysteries of the incarnation that was to last fifteen minutes. He spoke with focus, confidence, and an ease that belied his youthfulness. Standing still on his mark, he used broad, natural gestures, enthralling eye contact, and a gentle, clear voice. You could see in his soft-featured face the earnestness with which he spoke. His words did not falter; his memory did not fail him. Resolutely and gently, he proceeded through the well-known address. No other noises were heard during the period of his speech. For a quarter hour, the life of the village was suspended in the hushed expanse of the great church as the child's sweet voice echoed among its porticos and arches. The language of his oration was a Majorcan dialect of Catalan. I understood not a word. But I was enfolded into the drama of this humble village's celebration.

Though vastly different, a common element unifies these two events that enabled the participants to be drawn together in spite of dissimilarities in setting, background, experience, and language. What allowed the symbols to function so well is that they were executed with *excellence*. The performances did not draw attention to themselves but drew the listeners and participants together into the experience of something new. In each instance, the presence of Christ was manifest as the people gathered and as God's Word was delivered through Scripture, song, ritual, and oration.

In the first three chapters we have considered the meaning of art, its place in worship, the nature of performance and performatory language, and the need for worship leaders and preachers to perform in ways that disclose God's promise and presence. With these as the warp and weft, I will conclude the first part of this book by attempting to weave these theological threads into a coherent pattern. The unifying postulation is that when preachers and worship leaders attend to the matters of symbol and performance and handle their roles with aesthetic sensitivity, worship will be most effective. The key to aesthetic sensitivity is excellence.

STRIVING TO EXCEL

Excellence is sought in every field. It is encouraged by writers of dozens of books dealing with everything from *a* to *z*, from auto repair to the zymurgy. In recent years some of these books have become bestsellers—for example, *In Search of Excellence: Lessons from America's Best-Run Companies*, by Robert H. Waterman. It would not be an exaggeration to say that the topic of excellence has been so widely discussed as to make it cliché. In her *Handbook for Academic Authors*, Beth Luey warns that writers should avoid "trendy language which rapidly becomes overused and then dated."[1] She cites the word "excellence" as her first example.

Yet the pursuit of excellence is not exhausted. It is to be encouraged and is needed if ever people are to do things well, to achieve anything significant, to do more than make do. In worship and preaching, we want to do more than make do with what can be easily accomplished or readily acquired. In matters of faith, it seems there ought to be some compulsion to do things as well as we can. Why?

It is often said that we do our best in worship and in matters of faith because we should always bring our best to God. Our Creator deserves and demands the choicest of what we were created to be. As a rationale for excellence in relation to the performance of worship, prayer, and preaching, this assertion has little to support it. In fact, it is often the opposite that we bring to God in worship and are glad to be able to offer it. God does not demand our best. If that were the criterion for assembling in God's presence and engaging in the liturgical dialogue, few would have the confidence to gather or to speak. In the same way that we do not come to receive Holy Communion only when we feel worthy, we do not come to God with petitions or offerings of praise only when we have crafted them into their finest presentational form. We come to God in prayer and praise when we have a need to do so. That need may be spontaneous, as in the eruption of applause at the conclusion of an impassioned sermon. Or it may be a need that is so deeply felt and so achingly wrought that it comes forth only as a Spirit-borne sigh. In moments of weakness, we do not know how to pray as we ought; at such times we are unable to adorn our petitions with beautiful words and excellent turns of phrase. God does not demand that we do. God hears our prayer and praise however and whenever they are rendered. God even blesses our poorest sermons with the presence of the Spirit. Karl Barth reminds us that preaching is always a human action and that "humans beings are neither capable nor worthy of God."[2] Preaching is merely "an attempt," he says, one

> that is made with human means. In all circumstances it is made, then, with inadequate means. There is nothing here upon which to rely. But, through God, who raises up the dead, who calls into being that which is not, this attempt, this action, is undertaken as a (generally) *good work* insofar as it takes place under God's command and promise and blessing.[3]

It is not God who is impressed with human excellence.

Neither does God make distinction between those who can perform with excellence and those who do not have the skills to do so. Directors of church choirs know the truth of this. Every volunteer choir has, it seems, at least one eager singer who does not know how to guide his or her voice according to the dictates of the music or the canons of tonality. "Who is that off-key voice in the alto section?" listeners will remark, or "One of those baritones sounds as if he couldn't carry a tune in a bucket." The church choir director faces a dilemma. If the errant singers are filled with joy and participate with enthusiasm, it is hard to dismiss them from the group whose responsibility it is to bring vitality to the praise of the assembly. Church choir directors also know the truth of this conundrum: Often it is the least able voice that is the most filled with praise, for the ungifted singer is most grateful for the chance to enter the musical realm inhabited by the better gifted. Even poor singers love to sing and are happy to praise God with the voice they are given. Let it be remembered that the only word in Scripture on the issue of execution in vocal performance is given in the psalms, and there repeatedly: "Make a joyful noise unto God." No mention is made of singing in tune or with any particular beauty. So, what shall we make of the eager but discordant voice in a choir?

Or what of a children's choir that sings earnestly but without consensus as to pitch or key? That is praise, too. Joyful noises are not always pleasant. At least, they are not pleasant to us who endure them. They are, on the other hand, probably exceedingly pleasant to the God who created them in all their glorious inconsistency. Does God, one wonders, take any greater delight in the sweet weeping of the whippoorwill than in the abrasive braying of the ass?

Why sing with excellence? Why lead worship well? Why practice the sermon and speak in clear, precise, poetic language? Why strive to excel? The answer is not that God demands our best. God is pleased with that which is genuine over that which is perfected. As the psalmist advises us, it is the fruit of our brokenness that is most acceptable to God: "The sacrifice acceptable to God is a broken spirit; a broken and contrite heart, O God, you will not despise" (51:17).

Yet there is a reason to pursue excellence in matters of worship and preaching. It has to do not with God's expectations of us but with our expectations of one another and the ways that our modes of expression function. When we come to worship we gather as the Body of Christ to engage in rituals that are filled with art. We express ourselves with presentational symbols in the architecture and visual art that surround us, the movement and music that envelop us, the words of Scripture and sermon that enlighten us, and the language of prayer and praise that declares the contents of our hearts. We expect that in the presence of the gathering and the symbols at least three things will happen. First, the aesthetic symbols will enable us to express ourselves of things that are deeply felt and enable us to be in solidarity with those around us as well as with others who are or have been part of the body of believers. Second, the presence of the hidden God will be revealed to us through the careful leadership of those who preach, pray, and lead in worship. Third, the words we use in prayer, praise, and preaching will provide us access to God's power as God is with us and active for us. If these things are to be accomplished in our gatherings, then care must be given to the crafting and presentation of symbols that carry such important freight. Art is the train on which these expectations ride. The reason to execute the symbols of worship with excellence is to enable the presentational symbols of architecture, visual art, music, dance, drama, poetry, Scripture, and sermon to function freely and effectively among God's people.

Because all of our attempts at prayer, praise, and preaching are born of human effort and therefore inadequate, God is present to them and in them by God's choice. Like the braying of so many asses, even our attempts at worship, however inadequate, may be cherished by God. It is not because of any beauty we bring to these attempts that God chooses to inhabit them. God inheres in our symbols simply as a matter of grace. Therefore, the art that we pour into worship is created not for God's sake. Nor, as we have seen, is it for art's sake.

The art of worship is created for the people's sake and for the sake of their faith. We take pains to make worship artful because deep needs have to be addressed; because God speaks to us and knows us at our most sentient depths; because we seek unity in faith and solidarity with other members of the Body of Christ; because we wish to meet Jesus in the symbols that surround us; and because we are custodians of words that have such power as to create praise, bring blessing, bear forgiveness, proclaim promise, and shape thoughts that are too deep for words. If the art is not well executed, God won't suffer. But worshipers will.

The many who gather rely on worship leaders to do their jobs effectively, that is, with aesthetic sensitivity. When they fail, it is at the risk of forcing on the assembly's attention the faultiness of the few rather than leading the people toward a disclosure of the Hidden One. If the hymns are played too swiftly or too loudly, the opportunity for praise is supplanted by frustration at being rushed or drowned out by the organist. If Scripture is read by a person who has not studied the text and taken care as to pronunciation, diction, mood, and genre, the reader's inadequate preparation is forced on the attention of the listener. If the choir sings a song that has been insufficiently rehearsed, it draws attention to the poor planning of the director and to the embarrassment of the singers who are forced to attempt what they are ill prepared to accomplish. The preacher who speaks woodenly, obtusely, or with clumsy language challenges both the listeners in their desire to meet Jesus in the sermon and the Spirit, on whose presence we rely in order for the promise to be manifest. If the best preaching is only an attempt to speak God's promise, then our poorer efforts require greater grace to achieve a spiritual effect. God may choose to be present in poor preaching, but that is not a warrant for the preacher to practice indolence so that grace may abound.

The quality that is achieved when preachers and worship leaders perform their roles with excellence is transparency. They who are visible become hidden so that the Hidden One can be disclosed through their performance. The form of the Divine shows through what they say and do. There is, in true excellence, the quality of hiddenness. For Dietrich Bonhoeffer, hiddenness is the sign of genuine discipleship.

THE HIDDEN DISCIPLE

In *The Cost of Discipleship*, Dietrich Bonhoeffer paints a portrait of the person who seeks Jesus and is willing to pay the price for following him. God's grace is not cheap, Bonhoeffer warns, and those who desire to be disciples must bear the cost of lives that are changed and challenged by the gospel. At the center of Bonhoeffer's exploration of the Christian life lies a paradox. The Christian disciple is one who lives a "peculiar" or "extraordinary" life insofar as he or she brings light to the world and lives according to a rule of utter love. At the same time, as the disciple's work shines in the world, the disciple is in the dark as to the fact that he or she is doing any good thing at all. The disciple's works are hidden.

The idea of hiddenness in discipleship derives from the sixth chapter of Matthew, a portion of which stands as the epigraph to this chapter. "When you give alms," Jesus teaches, "do not let your left hand know what your right hand is doing" (6:3). Likewise, a few verses later Jesus says "when you fast, put oil on your head . . . so that your fasting may be seen not by others but by your Father who is in secret; and your Father who sees in secret will reward you" (6:17–18). To follow Jesus is to live charitably and devoutly. But, in doing so, Bonhoeffer counsels, the disciple encounters a danger: "The call to the 'extraordinary' is the inevitable risk [people] must take when they follow Christ. And therefore Jesus warns us to take heed."[4] The motive of the disciple must be something more than self-reflection. Love is not given for its own sake nor for the sake of ostentation. "Of course it has to be visible, but [disciples] must take care that it does not become visible simply for the sake of becoming visible."[5] The primary aim of love is to follow Jesus. Here, says Bonhoeffer, is the paradox:

> Our activity must be visible, but never be done for the sake of making it visible. "Let your light so shine before [others]" . . . and yet: Take care that you hide it! . . . That which is visible must also be hidden. The awareness on which Jesus insists is intended to prevent us from reflecting on our extraordinary position. We have to take heed that we do not take heed of our own righteousness. Otherwise the "extraordinary" which we achieve will not be that which comes from following Christ, but that which springs from our own will and desire.[6]

To resolve the paradox, we are driven to a hard task. We let our light be seen by others for the sake of Christ. But we hide our actions from *ourselves*. "Our task is simply to keep on following, looking only to our Leader who goes on before, taking no notice of ourselves or of what we are doing. We must be unaware of our own righteousness, and see it only in so far as we look unto Jesus. . . ."[7] To accomplish this, the disciple becomes a servant of Christ, looking only to him, adhering only to his example, standing in the shadow of the cross. In this way, the disciple's "obedience, following and love are entirely spontaneous and unpremeditated."[8] If one does good but is not unconscious of it, that person is simply displaying his or her own virtue. But the Christian lives in a state of voluntary blindness for the sake of Christ who is the source of all virtue.

What Bonhoeffer offers as a model for Christian life is also a guide for those who preach, lead, and offer public prayer in worship. Here, too, is an obvious quality of visibility. The few who are trained to lead others in worship take turns in taking stage. Some hold center place for a few moments, others for extended periods. Some conduct their roles in the shadows; others ascend pulpits and perform around the altar. The visibility of preachers, presiders, cantors, choirs, and other ministers cannot be avoided. But their roles can be managed in ways that avoid drawing unnecessary attention to their service. The self-conscious action of a minister forces itself on the focus of the assembly. It happens whether it results from a lack of confidence or from pride. Nothing, William J. Beeners is reported to have said, is more offensive than listening to preachers listen to themselves. But when ministers perform well, with ease, grace, confidence, and humility, their actions are perceived as fitting, natural, helpful, even necessary; not as a signal of self-importance or a magnet for recognition.

Taking our lead from Bonhoeffer's insight as to this paradox of discipleship, we can proceed to consider those attributes of aesthetic sensitivity that are the qualities of the hidden disciple.

THE HALLMARKS OF HIDDENNESS

When preachers and worship leaders perform their roles well, they are transparent. There is a hiddenness to excellence. Beyond the mechanics of execution relating to their performative roles, however, there are qualities that distinguish people who know how to subdue their visibility in worship for the sake of those who come to see Jesus. They include at least four traits: servanthood, diligence, authenticity, and humility.

The hidden disciple is a servant of God. Preachers are, in Bonhoeffer's sense of the word, extraordinary: called to proclaim Presence and promise in the sermon. They sit in their study, pore over the Scriptures, and reflect theologically on the ancient texts as they intersect with current situations. Then, they choose, according to the logical rightness and necessity of expression, the words and phrases that will be the conveyance of Christ's manifestation. If the preacher has worked diligently and successfully, it will be noticed. When the sermon shines forth with the light of Christ, there is no getting around the risk that the peripheral edge of illumination will fall on the preacher. The one who holds the candle is the one most likely to be bathed in its glow. The same can be said of other worship ministers. They are extraordinarily visible among the many. How can the few who are so distinguished avoid the danger of being visible? With what attitude can they maintain a hidden quality?

Paul instructed the Corinthian church in similar matters:

Indeed, the body does not consist of one member but of many. If the foot would say, "Because I am not a hand, I do not belong to the body," that would not make it any less a part of the body. And if the ear would say, "Because I am not an eye, I do not belong to the body," that would not make it any less a part of the body. If the whole body were an eye, where would the hearing be? If the whole body were hearing, where would the sense of smell be? . . .The eye cannot say to the hand, "I have no need of you," nor again the head to the feet, "I have no need of you." On the contrary, the members of the body that seem to be weaker are indispensable, and those members of the body that we think less honorable we clothe with greater honor, and our less respectable members are treated with greater respect; whereas our more respectable members do not need this. But God has so arranged the body, giving the greater honor to the inferior member, that there may be no dissension within the body, but the members may have the same care for one another. If one member suffers, all suffer together with it; if one member is honored, all rejoice together with it. Now you are the body of Christ and individually members of it. (1 Cor. 12:14–27)

No part of the Body of Christ, however visible, is greater than other parts. All together are equal members of the body of believers and servants of God. When the Body of Christ engages in service, the range of spiritual gifts abounds and each performs according to its function. In the service of worship, the gifts of the few join together with the gifts of the many and the Hidden One is disclosed among them. Some of the nomenclature of worship implies a heirarchy of duties: "leader," "presider," and "preacher" (from the Latin *praedicator*, with the prefix *prae* meaning "before" in terms of time, place, order, or degree). But preachers and leaders do not stand *before* the assembly in exalted roles. They stand, rather, *with* the assembly. The term *minister*, which applies equally to all who gather, renders an appropriate understanding of Paul's injunction. To *minister* is to *serve*. All parts of the body serve together to make it function; all members of the worshiping body minister together and to one another. No one part is more important than another, though certainly, a few will plan and prepare for the gathering of the many. The hidden servant in worship is one who plans and prepares carefully so that his or her role is not highlighted in the glare of inept performance. Nor do leaders, presiders, and preachers who wish to be hidden attempt to highlight their already extraordinary roles by seeking to dance beyond the shadows into the radiance of Christ's light. The servant performs in the shadows, doing what is necessary and doing it well, so that the source of light is seen, is seen clearly, and is not obstructed.

The hidden disciple is diligent. Hiding is not easy. As a child, my brother used to take delight in being the person who was never found in the game "Hide and Seek." Because we lived on a farm, he was able to slip away and crawl into diabolically clever inglenooks of space. He would burrow inside the machinery of the combine or twine his thin limbs around rafters in the dark reaches of a shed. I knew the territory of the farm as well as he did. But I could not find him if he chose to work at being hidden.

In the extraordinary roles of worship leadership, ministers must also work at being hidden. If all preaching and worship leadership is, at best, an attempt, then our efforts need to be made with care and with the prayer that God inspire them.

As with any art, in matters of verbal expression there are some who are especially gifted. In Christian service, these gifts are born of the Spirit. Paul speaks repeatedly of the spiritual endowments of the Body of Christ. For example, "And God has appointed in the church first apostles, second prophets, third teachers; then deeds of power, then gifts of healing, forms of assistance, forms of leadership, various kinds of tongues" (1 Cor. 12:28). But spiritual giftedness is not a substitute for diligence. It is never sufficient to rely on the impressiveness of one's spiritual powers in the accomplishment of the important roles of worship leadership. Those who can pray with eloquence ought not to rely overly on the genius of the moment to supply them with their words. Preachers who are gifted orators must not trust in their creative skills as an excuse for insufficient study, reflection, and craftwork.[9] Worship leaders who are blessed with a commanding and graceful liturgical presence should prepare for their roles with as much care as those for whom such movement and speech come with difficulty. "Since you are eager for spiritual gifts," Paul advises, "strive to *excel* in them for building up the church" (1 Cor. 14:12, italics mine). Striving to excel in preaching and worship leadership means going beyond the rudiments of sermon craft or prayer composition. It means taking extra steps to create verbal expression that reaches deeply and resonates with the worshiping assembly. Those extra steps include working and reworking the language of our liturgical expression and practicing our parts as any performing artist does. The importance of going beyond the basics to consider matters of performance is forcefully underscored by Charles Bartow. In speaking to preachers and the readers of Scripture, he says:

> to work at developing imaginative, empathic, vocal, and physical gestural virtuosity is not to devote time to what is beside the point. Nor is it only to give attention to a matter of secondary importance, mere technical drill, that may help us to get across to others what we have, by other means, acquired for ourselves. It is, instead, to condition one's total self (not just one's mind through study, but also one's body through drill) as a site for acquisition of knowledge. It is to hone the ways by which we come to experience and understand presence and The Presence.[10]

Some of the artistic means that can be practiced and employed with diligence by preachers and leaders of prayer and worship will be discussed in part 2 of this book. But one of the matters of diligence that relates to all of these extraordinary attempts can be addressed here: The hidden disciple is diligent in prayer.

How is it that God blesses our efforts at preaching and disclosing Christ in worship? It is something that is outside our ability to control. We may attempt to create words and worship that are meaningful and may fail miserably because of the ways we choose to live our lives outside church. If God hates our solemn assemblies as God did in Amos's day, no amount of cleverness or skill will bring God back into that which God chooses to abandon. Only one thing can accomplish that: prayer. One of the great gifts of the Old Testament is the reminder that God's mind can be changed by prayer. On the other hand, if our attempts at preaching and worship seem feeble and clumsy, we might assume that God would choose to be absent from them. Here again, God's presence does not rely on our ability or choice. It is precisely in our moments of weakness that God intercedes for us with the Holy Spirit. Because God's presence in our words and in our worship is never based on our initiative, we simply pray that God's promises will be fulfilled in our attempts to disclose the One who is hidden. Karl Barth, who labeled our ministerial endeavors as mere attempts, provides us with a consummating affirmation that emphasizes the need for prayer. "Preaching, then," and to this I would add all worship leadership, "must become prayer. It must," he says,

> turn into seeking and invoking of God, so that ultimately everything depends upon whether God hears and answers our prayer. . . .There is no place, then, for a victorious confidence in the success of our own action, but only for a willingness to open ourselves to heaven and to remain open to God, so that God himself can now come to us and give us all things richly. Our attitude then, must be controlled from above: nothing from me, all things from God, no independent achievement, only dependence on God's grace and will.[11]

Our trust that God is a part of all that we do and say in worship comes as a result of our diligence in prayer; *the vocation of the few is invocation of the One*, seeking God's presence, promise, and performance in our assemblies.

The hidden disciple is authentic. The character of those who speak in public has been an object of consideration since Aristotle undertook the study of rhetoric in the fourth century B.C. It continues to be a critical issue. As the past century was coming to a close, the people of the United States found that they had to weigh carefully the words of a president who had admitted to numerous public lies. In spite of the president's popular stance on issues, the message of his oratory was veiled by inauthenticity. Preachers and leaders of worship face the same standard of judgment. Their message is obscured, perhaps even belied, when focus bears on the issue of their trustworthiness. But the meaning of their discourse is disclosed when their faithfulness and integrity are given.

Excellence in preaching, prayer, and worship leadership involves at least seven qualities of authenticity. They reveal the truth about the gospel promise, the genuineness of the preacher, and an honest appraisal of the congregational context. Authentic preachers and worship leaders are people who speak with honesty, simplicity, kerygmatic centeredness, conviction, contextuality, originality, and creativity.

Hidden disciples express themselves in language that is honest to their character. When the speaker reaches to grasp for language that is lofty or arcane, it does little to draw people into prayer, praise, or an understanding of the Scriptures. Such language tends to draw people into contemplation of its meaning, confusion, and either admiration of or frustration with the one who chose the words. Similarly, the speaker who bends down to find words that are at the most common level of understanding will be visible for having stooped low. The speaker is also conspicuous who stretches for words that seem properly religious or patently pious. Authentic speakers will use words that are true to their own patterns of expression and piety. From the lips of certain persons, the use of the Old English "thou" and "thy" in prayer fall genuinely on the listeners' ears. From others, they sound contrived. Preachers and worship leaders should craft their language from words that are natural and accessible. Natural language allows for the disciple to remain hidden. It is the distraction of reaching that is noticeable, as if one were grasping for a thesaurus or an ancient prayer book.

Hidden preachers and worship leaders express themselves with simplicity. Even when the erudition of the speaker is genuine and can be presented honestly and without reach, it is a service to the gospel and to the assembly to render the dialogue simply. Overusing the language of learning is a mistake often made by young preachers. In critique of my early sermons, my wife would comment, "It sounds as if you are preaching to a church full of college professors." In my naïveté, I mistook her judgment as a compliment. What better speakers learn is the wealth of expression that resides in the uncommon use of common language.

The expression of hidden disciples is centered in the kerygma. The meaning of this Greek word used so often by Paul (κήρυγμα) is proclamation or preaching. But its use by Paul in the epistles suggests a range of meaning. C. H. Dodd analyzed Paul's use of kerygma in *The Apostolic Preaching and Its Development*, published in 1937. In discussing the primitive preaching of the early church, Dodd draws together the range of what Paul implies by its use:

The prophecies are fulfilled, and the new Age is inaugurated by the
coming of Christ.
He was born of the seed of David.
He died according to the Scriptures, to deliver us out of the present
evil age.
He was buried.
He rose on the third day according to the Scriptures. He is exalted at
the right hand of God, as Son of God and Lord of quick and dead.
He will come again as judge and savior of men.[12]

Preaching, prayer, and worship that are kerygmatic are those which hold
Christ at their center and disclose him through the revelation of these biblical images. Just as the Paschal Candle stands in the center of the assembly,
Christ himself stands at the center of the gathering and all focus bears on him.
The hidden worship leader or preacher is one who serves so as to disclose this
kerygmatic presence and does not eclipse it. This means that the themes of
worship and sermon are always biblical themes and not personal themes.
Kerygmatic authenticity suggests that preachers and worship leaders subju-
gate their personalities and preferences to the primacy of the gospel. Thus,
sermons are not to be political diatribes or turgid expositions of personal
opinion. And prayers are not to be misguided missiles aimed at the assembly.
The focus in all parts of worship is to converge on the Presence and the
promise.

The hidden disciple is convicted by the gospel. This means that preachers
and worship leaders speak and act in ways that reveal that they have been
authentically touched and claimed by the working of the Holy Spirit. Their
words ring true because they know the truth of the promise for themselves.
They stand as witness to what God can do and wishes to do among God's people. Furthermore, they lead with the conviction that God's people are called
to repentance and are assured of the forgiveness of their sins. Yet bold testimony and definitive proclamation remain hidden because they point to the
One who stands at the center of the liturgical interchange.

The hidden servant of the gospel is aware of context. Like the prophecy of
ancient Israel, God's Word for us is always a word for a particular time and
place. The particulars of each service of worship change as much with geographical location as with the procession of time through the weeks on the cal-
endar or the movement of the minute hand on the clock. In other words, the
context is always changing. Sermons, prayers, and exclamations of praise that
are fitting in one time and place will be ill-fitting in another.[13] The authentic
preacher and leader of worship will be attuned to the special circumstances of
each worship moment; they will lead and speak properly for each occasion.
That is, in the *ordinary* patterns of worship they will intersperse material that

is *proper* for the many in the moment. The propers are not merely prescribed rubrics to be found in a worship manual. They are found in the gathering and cued by the particularities of each gathering. The 8:00 A.M. service has a different constituency than the 11:00 service. United Methodist churches in Minnesota have different rhythms than those in California. Lutheran worshipers in North Dakota have different concerns and needs than those in Leipzig or Ethiopia. To be blind to the subtle differences in context makes for infelicities of expression that are a hindrance to kerygmatic disclosure. To be aware of particularities and to respond according to them is a delicate, but effective, element of good performance.

The authentic servant is hidden through originality. If preachers and worship leaders are aware of the particularities of each context, they will prepare their liturgical expression accordingly. They will also be prepared to make changes as the circumstances change. This suggests, of course, that the material is fresh and born of the preacher's and the worship leader's struggle with text (biblical text and liturgical text) and context. It does not mean that they will avoid seeking assistance from commentaries and worship helps. But, in the end, the words they use to express the promise of God and the concerns of the people will be their own words. Except in special circumstances,[14] preachers would not dare to deliver, and certainly never take credit, for another writer's sermon. Effective sermons are crafted to fit the setting and are fluid, ready to shift as the need may arise. I have seen preachers deal unexpectedly, but effectively, with the sudden crack of thunder, the deafening cry of an infant tantrum, even the angered harangue of a listener who chose the preaching moment as the time to upbraid preacher and assembly for perceived grievances. Prayers and other liturgical language can also be original and crafted just as carefully, with contextual authenticity and fluidity, as the sermon.

Last, the hidden disciple demonstrates authenticity through creative expression. As we have seen, it is the use of presentational symbols that allows for language to reach deeply and create resonance between speaker and listener. Deep calls to deep through artistic channels. This suggests the need for imaginative ways of speaking and performing. Patterns of language and images that once seemed fresh can become worn and frayed with use. As symbols become cliché, they lose their ability to lead us through layers of meaning; they no longer surprise us or help us to see something new. But our language is rich and the combinations of words and images is inexhaustible. Creative use of language yields figures that provide people with new perspectives on an old story. Creativity of expression is especially important as we try to move beyond traditional heirarchical language for the sake of inclusivity. When the few prepare for the sake of the many to speak and lead in ways that disclose the Hidden One, fresh language, new metaphors, and creative configurations of forms will enliven the liturgical dialogue.

Creative language is not only new, it is also unique. All people express themselves with singularity of style. The authentic preacher and leader of worship will not simply look to duplicate the innovative language of others but will attempt to create their own expressions, assemble new images, and open the eyes of auditors and worshipers to the perception of new worlds that derive from the unique perspective and experience of their own lives. Just as consideration of the congregational context is a quality of authenticity, so is the employment of the unique context of the individual whereby the person's spiritual gifts and personal experiences are brought together in service to the gospel.

The hidden disciple is humble. I once had the opportunity to invite a renowned preacher and homiletician to preach at a synodical assembly. I wasn't asking much: just that he come to speak to the assembled pastors about the importance of their role as preachers and then, by way of example, deliver for them the best sermon that they ever heard. Our speaker warily accepted the invitation and prepared well to meet the criteria I had outlined. As I listened to the sermon that evening, I was struck by a number of performative considerations. First, the sermon was well crafted and rich with evocative language, figurative speech, and illustrative material. Second, it had fine conceptual content with perhaps a bit more theological substance than is usually heard in churches because the audience was theologically trained. Third, in spite of my objectivity and evaluative attitude, I was drawn in by the sermon and enwrapped in the world it created. I entered, as the preacher intended, a world that was real enough to live in.[15] In that world, I was brought closer to Christ. The preacher was extraordinarily visible, not only in Bonhoeffer's sense of the term, but also because his presence in the assembly was amplified. His voice was broadcast through dozens of speakers, and his physical image was projected onto a huge screen that made his movements and facial gestures visible to all in the arena. Nonetheless, the large presence of the preacher was not the predominant image. It was merely the window through which Christ entered to walk among us. In reflecting on that sermon, I could not set aside the realization that the preacher did a fine job. He was visible in having performed well. But what was it that, in spite of the impressiveness of the presentation, drew me in and allowed for the promise to be heard? It was the humility with which the speaker performed.

There is a transparency to genuine humility. It grows out of a desire to serve the Word and emulate the One who is the Word. "Do nothing from selfish ambition or conceit," Paul says,

> but in humility regard others as better than yourselves. Let each of you
> look not to your own interests, but to the interests of others. Let the
> same mind be in you that was in Christ Jesus, who, though he was in
> the form of God, did not regard equality with God as something to be
> exploited, but emptied himself, taking the form of a slave, being born
> in human likeness. And being found in human form, he humbled him-
> self and became obedient to the point of death—even death on a cross.
> (Phil. 2:3–8)

When servants are humbled through obedience, they lay self aside that Christ
may be revealed.

The opposite state is hubris. It, too, is transparent, but what hubris discloses
is not the Hidden One. Pride discloses the need of the self for recognition. It
speaks, oftentimes, more loudly than the prepared words of the speaker or
worship leader. Because of the preeminence of pride, hubristic preachers and
worship leaders will fail in their attempts at hiddenness and force on the attention of worshipers their need for adulation. What is seen is not Christ but the
raw, unfettered ego of the minister, inflated to mask his or her anxieties.

Humility lays aside the self and acknowledges that the human attempt to
preach or lead in worship is inadequate if it is not inspired by God. "Preaching has to take place in humility and soberness," advises Karl Barth again,

> and as the prayer of those that realize that God himself must confess
> their human word if it is to be God's Word. Here is the point . . . where
> it opens up to heaven, and, standing before the mystery of the gracious
> God, we confess that it is not in our power that our human word
> should be God's Word.[16]

While laying aside the self in service to the Word, humility also acknowledges that God has given gifts to be used in that service. The gifts are many
and, in some cases, extraordinary. The speaker mentioned above had uncommon skills for preaching. Artists and musicians who see themselves as ministers of the Word also acknowledge the source and range of their giftedness.
When they perform in *soli Deo gloria*, they honor the gift of creativity by offering their inventions to the Creator. As I have said, their artistic gifts are rendered not for the sake of pleasing a demanding God, but for the sake of those
who worship and for the sake of resonating in their creative capacity with the
Source of all creation. In striving for excellence and capitalizing on the talents
they have been given, artistic ministers are acknowledging the wellspring of
their talents and are using them to connect others as well as themselves with
that generative source. Here again, the self is set aside so that the gift may benefit others and honor the Giver. When artists excel, that is, when they perform
to their fullest potential, they are doing what they were created to do and being
who they were made to be. They reveal through their efforts the infinite and

undiminishing creative capacity of the One who is still present and active in the cosmos.

At this point, we come full circle and arrive back at the paradox that Bonhoeffer identified as the challenge of discipleship. Gifted ministers will want to share their gifts and will, consequently, be visible. But, if they are filled with humility, their gifts will not be conspicuous; only the Giver will.

EXCELLENCE IS NOT PERFECTION

Do the perfect thing: make some mistakes. One of the biggest mistakes you can make is to try not to make any mistakes. However hard you work at doing everything right, sometimes you'll say the wrong word or make the wrong move. You're only human. And it's precisely your humanity that makes you approachable and believable. So relax and be natural. Your goofs will also signal an important truth: there is a limit to your dependability. No one should ever put their entire trust in you. There is only One worthy of such trust.[17]

This practical advice was given by Pastor James E. Miller to his daughter Christine on the occasion of her ordination into the ministry. His counsel is instructive for all who would seek to preach and lead in prayer and public worship. Although we seek excellence and strive to make the most of the talents God has given us in service of the gospel and for the sake of God's people, we do not presume to be perfect or seek to become perfectionists.

Perfectionism, as I mean it here, is not simply the attempt to do things well or to imitate the goodness of Christ. It is the uncompromising pursuit of flawless execution. Excellence suggests doing one's best and trusting that God will use our gifts to accomplish God's purpose. The perfectionist is not satisfied with doing one's best and is unyielding in critical judgment.

I once noticed a beautiful guitar sitting in the corner of a friend's living room. "I didn't know you played the guitar," I said.

"I used to, but I don't anymore," my friend replied.

"Why not? Weren't you good at it?"

"Yes, actually, I was quite good. I worked at it for fifteen years," he admitted.

"Then, why did you give it up?" I asked.

"Because, as good as I had become, I finally realized that I would never be able to play as well as Segovia. I just didn't have his talent. So, I figured, why waste any more time?" "Play skillfully on the strings," the psalmist declares (33:3), but this man's skill was silenced by inflexible measurement against an impossible standard.

Perfectionism is not the same thing as excellence. Excellence, in service of the gospel, acknowledges human limitation. It admits to the fact that all preaching, prayer, and praise are imperfect. They are merely attempts to engage in liturgical dialogue and to disclose God's presence and promise. They succeed not by our skill or faultless execution. They succeed only by God's choosing to inhere in the symbols we choose for liturgical expression. If we assume that God will choose to be present among us only when our worship is flawless, then we place impossible demands on the ministers while we deny the freedom of God to inspire and bless our attempts at proclamation and praise. The Spirit is not hindered by our denial of God's freedom to be with us in imperfect prayer and praise. Again, it is precisely in our weakness that the Spirit intercedes for us with sighs too deep for words.

Perfectionism is twice unbecoming a minister of the gospel. First, it is unforgiving. Jesus said:

> You have heard that it was said, "You shall love your neighbor and hate your enemy." But I say to you, Love your enemies and pray for those who persecute you, so that you may be children of your Father in heaven; for he makes his sun rise on the evil and on the good, and sends rain on the righteous and on the unrighteous. For if you love those who love you, what reward do you have? Do not even the tax collectors do the same? And if you greet only your brothers and sisters, what more are you doing than others? Do not even the Gentiles do the same? Be perfect, therefore, as your heavenly Father is perfect. (Matt. 5:43–48)

Be perfect, Jesus adjures. With what kind of perfection? God is, as Jesus makes clear, perfect in love. To love as God loves means that we will be charitable when the world says to hate and beneficent to those who wrong us. Being perfect in love means that we are forgiving as God is forgiving toward us. Here is where being perfect, as Jesus instructs, and perfectionism are at cross purposes. Perfectionism suggests that someone serve as judge and critic, whether it is in evaluation of his or her own performance or that of others. Because it holds the model of faultless performance up as the standard and measures unstintingly against it, it tends to be unforgiving. It is, therefore, implicitly *imperfect.* "Be perfect," Jesus says, and with perfect love, be accepting of faults and forgiving, both of self and of others.

Second, seeking perfection is wrong because it is a form of idolatry. As Pastor Miller advised, only God is capable of flawless dependability. Perfectionism suggests that there is a certain impeccability in the one who judges the performance of others. But, since there is no perfection except in God or through Christ, to raise oneself to this level of judgment is to expect more of oneself than can be delivered; though we attempt to imitate him, we are not Christ and no one is completely godly. Perfectionist critique raises up the critic as all-knowing and ever-demanding; in this, Christ is not revealed. What is revealed is the voice of the critic. To exalt oneself is opposite of what preachers and worship leaders are called to do. Their job is exclusively to elevate Christ.

Here, then, is excellence. We use the spiritual gifts that God gives us in service of the gospel and for the sake of God's people. While we acknowledge our insufficiency and weakness, we attempt to preach God's Word and lead God's people in prayer and praise, trusting that God will be present to us and active for us in the symbols we choose. By performing our tasks well and with aesthetic sensitivity, we remain hidden so that the hidden One is disclosed among us. Or, to put it in the poet's words, excellence in ministry is remembering who we are.

> We are workers, not master builders,
>   ministers, not messiahs.
> We are prophets of a future not our own.[18]

CONCLUSION

With this, we arrive at the completion of our theological task. The goal has been to consider certain aesthetic elements of liturgical expression, especially with regard to preaching, public prayer, and the various proper pronouncements that guide the worshiping assembly. In the first chapters we have examined three aesthetic issues. Chapter 1 dealt with the presentational quality of language and its capacity for speaking of things too deep for words and for creating resonance between people. The second chapter considered the presence and performance of the hidden God who is revealed through careful preaching and worship leadership. Chapter 3 looked at the performatory quality of liturgical language, which has the power to bind the assembly together in prayer and praise and which calls on God's power for blessing and the fulfillment of God's promises. In this chapter, we have seen how the aesthetic responsibility to create presentational, revelational, and performatory liturgical expression is accomplished through the pursuit of excellence in performing the roles of preacher and worship leader. Performing with excellence, that is, serving with diligence, authenticity, and humility, enables the minister to remain hidden so that the promise and presence of God can be disclosed.

What we have assembled is a theoretical framework for preachers and leaders of public prayer and worship that demonstrates the significance of the aesthetic dimensions of their roles. Those who undertake these roles have a responsibility to do them well, not because God demands that we perform with excellence, but because expressing ourselves well enables worship and preaching to move people, to transform their lives, and to draw them closer to God. We do things with excellence for the sake of the faith of those who come to worship to see Jesus.

Informed by this theological construction, we turn our attention now to practical matters. How does one select language that has presentational capacity? How do preachers create sermons that are so filled with virtual life that they appear as worlds real enough to enter? What kind of language enables and enlivens the three-way liturgical dialogue? How can preachers and leaders of public prayer and worship express themselves so as to serve as Philip to those who wish to see Jesus? With what language can they speak to draw people together in prayer and call on the power of God's promise and presence in worship? In part 2, we take up these practical issues, beginning first with the language of preaching.

PART 2

5

Treasure in Earthen Vessels

> For what we preach is not ourselves, but Jesus Christ as Lord, with
> ourselves as your servants for Jesus' sake. For it is the God who
> said, "Let light shine out of darkness," who has shone in our hearts
> to give the light of the knowledge of the glory of God in the face
> of Christ. But we have this treasure in earthen vessels, to show that
> the transcendent power belongs to God and not to us.
>
> *2 Cor. 4:5–7 RSV*

Proclamation is always a human endeavor. Even when God's message is delivered most directly and without explicit interpretation, as in the reading of
Scriptures, there are layers of intrinsic interpretation. At every stage of trans-
mission (collecting, editing, arranging, copying, translating, and publishing),
human effort has brought God's Word forth with theological judgment.
Today, when a person stands to read God's Word in worship, the reader continues to put fingerprints on it, making conscious or unconscious decisions
about the text's meaning by the way the reader handles the text. Everything
the reader does in the oral interpretation of the text reflects on its meaning for
the community gathered: every gesture, glance, pause; each variation in pace
and inflection; or the lack of attention to these things brings an element of
human judgment to the reading. The Word bears the marks of human interpretation every time it is proclaimed. In preaching, the human element is
explicit. The preacher moves from the text, through stages of understanding
and evaluation, to the point where God's Word is proclaimed to God's people
in a new moment. Ancient messages are interpreted for contemporary people,
and the universal shape of the human/divine encounter is reviewed in light of
current context. The treasure of God's Word is carried, to put it in Paul's
terms, in earthen vessels. What are these earthen vessels? Paul's metaphor is

clearly borrowed from the prophet who praises the creator, saying "we are the clay, and you are our potter; we are all the work of your hand" (Isa. 64:8). The earthen vessels are we who proclaim God's Word by speaking words of power, promise, and presence.

Proclamation puts a reverse twist on the biblical image. Whereas God is the potter and we are the clay, in proclamation we resonate with God's creativity by using our own creative powers to express the Word of God and disclose the Divine Presence. The Word becomes the raw material out of which we fashion modes of proclamation. Whether the vessels we now craft are as the crude clay of ancient pottery or the fine crystal of later technology, the treasure is always conveyed by the work of human hands and hearts. In other words, proclamation is art.

Having laid a theological foundation for understanding the aesthetic dimensions of liturgical expression in part 1, we turn now to considering the specific ways that preaching, public prayer, and the language of worship leadership are forms of art and the practical considerations that relate to their successful design and execution. This chapter will focus on the art of preaching and consider the components that go into the making of the pots and goblets that are human proclamation. Acknowledging the discursive property of preaching, we will consider the use of nondiscursive, or presentational, language in preaching. And we will look at what preachers can learn from poets regarding the use of ordinary language as it is put into extraordinary service as the preacher's words become the window through which Christ is seen and the door through which he enters to walk among God's assembled people.

PREACHING AS AN ART

Preaching is an art. This is widely, though not universally, agreed upon.[1] Yet, if we apply the same philosophical framework to the consideration of preaching as we do to other forms of art, we will see that it is indeed an art form.

Returning to the theoretical groundwork of chapter 1, it will be remembered that art is the creation of forms that are symbolic of human feeling. When a painter applies pigment to canvas, the artist is using combinations of color, light, shade, shape, line, and design to express something internal. What the painter expresses is ineffable, too complex and too deep for words. Yet the colors and forms of the painting are set forth as symbols that work together to express something of the knowledge of the inner life of the artist. These symbols are perceived by observers of the work and bring the viewers to an understanding of something new, something of the feelings and experience of the artist. As we have seen, the same process occurs in music, poetry, and in all forms of art. The artist selects symbols, according to the logical rightness and necessity of expression, and arranges them within the canons of the artistic medium to articulate those sentient things that the artist wishes to express. This aesthetic process also occurs in preaching. Preaching is the creation of symbols that give expression to the ineffable world that is vitally felt and experienced by the preacher. Because it is also the proclamation of promise, preaching has a theological component that other forms of art do not necessarily have. Preaching is kerygmatic: It is the preacher's attempt to create a form that, growing out of a scriptural text or biblical idea, expresses some aspect of what the preacher takes to be an important connection between God's Word and what is going on in the hearts and lives of God's people. By philosophical definition, preaching is art. Yet the question begs for clarification: What is the form of proclamation?

Clearly, proclamation takes many forms. In fact, when art is rendered for faith's sake, that is, when it is kerygmatic, it is always proclamation. Visual art preaches just as well as the verbal arts do, and music can have the effect of being doubly proclamatory, through the symbols of music and text. What Saint Augustine said about prayers that are sung can also be said of musical proclamation: The one who sings preaches twice. Thus, Johann Sebastian Bach can be known as the Fifth Evangelist even though he is not known for having preached God's Word in the discursive sense. His music is proclamation. It is filled with Christian symbolism rendered numerically and visually in his scores; his texts express an orthodoxy that is couched in deep spirituality; and the shape and texture of his melodies, counterpoint, and harmonies express a faith that resonates with believers today as well as they did in his lifetime. Proclamation can also take the form of sculpture, architecture, dance, even gesture. Recently I witnessed the power of the unspoken word as a dancer signed the words of a song being sung in worship. Although I could hear the music and its text, I imagined the heightened significance the signing would have for one who could not hear. I know the beauty that words can have; not only in their meanings, but also in the euphonic felicity of their selection and placement. But these gestured words had a new beauty, like the fluid movement of the heron's wings. In them was the music of motion, complete with rhythm, meter, shape, and phrasing. Although the literal content of the message was different than that which was sung (articles and conjunctions are often omitted in signing for the sake of synchronization), what was lost in literary nuance was made up for by the beauty of the poetic movement. When signing is used in this way, proclamation takes on a fresh form and presents itself in new dimensions to those who can hear as well as to those who cannot. Proclamation also takes many literary forms. In fact, all literary forms that are created for the sake of faith are forms of proclamation: God's promise has been proclaimed in novel, epic poetry, hymnody, drama, short story, and, of course, in sermon. The point being stressed here is that proclamation can take the form of any art, so long as it is created in service of the gospel. Insofar as human creativity is vast and varied, so too are the forms of proclamation. We place the treasure of God's promise in all types of earthen vessels. Proclamation is art for faith's sake.

Yet preaching, as it is usually conceived, is a literary art. For the preacher, one form of artistic symbol is predominant. Like the novelist, playwright, or writer of any kind, the preacher uses words and strings them together so as to give expression to the gospel message. Sermons may include set pieces from other forms, such as music, film, visual illustration, poetry, history, jokes, or quotations, but in the end, it is the preacher's choice of language that is the glue that binds the parts and sets. The words the preacher selects laminate the plies into a whole. Thus, preachers do what poets do: They are wordsmiths, careful choosers and users of language. And the sermon is a poetic form of art.

One can argue whether preaching is poetry. It all depends, of course, on your definition of poetry. Louise Rosenblatt contends that all types of literary art are poetry. She defines poetry as "the whole category of aesthetic transactions between readers and texts," without being concerned for the greater or lesser "poeticity" of a specific genre.[2] Gail Ramshaw prefers to say that most poetry lacks a communal sense of grounding that the language of worship must have. It is metaphoric, but because liturgy is the expression of all of God's people, "liturgy is not poetry."[3] In this sense, preaching, as a prominent part of liturgical expression, would not be considered poetry because it is expressive not of a singular perspective but reflective of a catholic voice. The predominant issue, however, is not whether we classify preaching as poetry (I would), but the use of language. What both of these writers understand is that literary arts depend on the use of language and that poetic language is abundant in good prose.

As a poetic form of art, preaching does what all poetry does. It creates an aura of illusion that sets itself apart from its immediate environment and engages the listener in an instance of virtual life.

THE ANCIENT MODE OF VIRTUAL REALITY

In 1995 Walt Disney Productions released a milestone film called *Toy Story*. It was the first successful[4] animated feature-length film created entirely from digital computer images. The Disney artists did not use pen, ink, paper, and paint to create the thousands of frames that make up the unfolding action of the movie as they had in most of their previous animated creations. For this film, they generated all the images and scenes using advanced computer graphics programming. The filmmakers offer a sly confession as to the nature of their craft by slipping a wordplay into one scene of the film. When the young protagonist's house goes on the market, the For Sale sign on the front lawn reveals the name of the film's fictitious real estate agency: "Virtual Realty."

The creation of virtual reality is thought to be an invention of the computer age. But it is, in fact, an ancient art. Creating virtual realms is what art has always been about. From chapter 1 we recall that philosopher Susanne K. Langer classifies this function as one of the identifying qualities of art. All art has the impression of illusion enfolding it. When one encounters a painting, the viewer is drawn into the work and loses awareness of the peripheral elements of reality that physically surround the work. The percipient's attention is suspended in a virtual realm that is a semblance of real space and the symbol of life. Like the Disney film or a virtual reality video game, there is something obviously not real about the medium. Yet the illusion is sufficient to dispel critical analysis of the form and to envelop the viewer in an aura of virtuality that has the shape of genuine experience.

We also considered in the first chapter the possibility that worship is a form of art that creates the illusion of virtual experience. Part of that illusion comes from the virtual reality of the sermon. The sermon, as a poetic form, does what all poetry does. It creates the sense of virtual life. Preaching develops a verbal world that seems real, convincing, and pertinent. And if it is successfully kerygmatic, it is also full of promise.

As we have seen, the question that informs the making of the poetic illusion is not "What is the poet trying to say or trying to make us feel?" but "What has the poet made and how has it been made?" The same kind of question can be asked of the preacher: "What has the preacher made and how has it been made?" If the sermon is successful in creating a world of pertinence and promise, then the preacher has made an illusion. Like poetry, it is the semblance of life. Fred Craddock describes it this way:

> By means of images the preaching occasion will be a re-creation of the way life is experienced now held under the light of the Gospel. Here imagination does not take off on flights of fantasy, but walks down the streets where we live.[5]

This leads to an important question. How does the sermon's sense of illusion function in a medium that is essentially discursive? How can the discourse of a sermon work presentationally? The preacher, like the poet, strings language together to create the illusion. The sermon becomes a presentational form when the words used are vivid, evocative, and imaginative. The words create images that have the power to evoke and resonate with the audience. They do not need to describe the feelings they want to evoke or the connections that they wish to make with the listeners. The preacher does not need to tell his or her audience that the sermon will have to do with sentient things like emotion or faith. Rather, through the imaginative use of language, the preacher symbolizes sentient things and establishes resonance with the listeners by virtue of the poetic illusion.

Yet the preacher is usually trying to do something more than create an illusion. The preacher is also proclaiming the promise and attempting to disclose the Divine Presence. This is accomplished not only through the use of language that engages but through language that conveys information, teaches, exhorts, and enlightens. There is both a literal and a poetic function in the discourse of preaching.

WHAT IS THE POINT?

There are, as we have seen, two functions of language. One is to stimulate feelings and attitudes in the hearer. The second is literal: to convey information. If one were to consider preaching's literal function, then it is fair to ask the question that poetic criticism avoids: "What is the preacher trying to say?" or "What is the sermon's point?" Although creating a work of art may be a part of what the preacher is attempting, he or she is also interested in bringing the listener to an understanding of the actual concepts being expressed. It is important for the audience not only to be moved but also to be taught, corrected, or made to understand. Part of the preacher's job is to allow for this to happen. But it is only one part. The preacher needs to keep both functions of language in mind to accomplish his or her whole task.

How do the two functions of language work together in preaching? If the preacher chose to make purely conceptual and informational expression his or her only goal in the sermon, it could be done in nonpoetic ways. The preacher could omit all colorful language, story, carefully turned phrases, emotion, and life. In this case, the preaching would be less a sermon than a lecture, designed with discursive economy to convey theological information. That which turns lecture material into an expressive form, into a sermon, is the enrichment of concepts and ideas with illustrations and vivid language, literary and poetic devices that make the sermon live. This is no mere decoration: It is the difference between lecture and life.

To ask the question of literal expression in preaching is to beg the question of preaching as a form of art. As Langer has said:

> The distinction between discursive and presentational symbols does
> not correspond to the difference between literal and artistic mean-

ings . . . for though the material of poetry is verbal, its import is not
the literal assertion made in works, but the way the assertion is made.[6]

What she says here of poetry is valid for preaching. Although one would not
subordinate the literal meaning of preaching to the artistic meaning, to claim
that preaching is an art is to acknowledge it as a form that has artistic significance in its power to create virtual life through the use of presentational language. The "literal assertions" of a sermon, important in their own right, play
the part of harmony in relation to the artistic meaning of the work. This is true
because it is the aesthetic component in preaching that engages the heart and
hews channels through which deep calls to deep.

An important question arises at this point. Is it true that preaching, as the
symbolic expression of sentience, is more profound than the mere literal
expression of concepts and information? Again, Langer is helpful: "It is not
true that whatever can be expressed symbolically can be expressed better
literally."[7] In other words, a more adequate rendering of a sermon would not
be to make it more conceptually and informationally explicit, but to make it
more poetic.

This is good news for preachers in two ways. First, it frees us from expecting that our sermons need to be intricate explications of biblical or theological themes. There are occasions—in fact, a great many occasions, perhaps as
many as one or two every week—when the preacher attempts to construct a
sermon in which the literal content is simple and straightforward. There are
issues of theology that are complex, to be sure. But, if they are to be the meat
of a sermon, they need to be digestible and delivered in manageable bites. And
there ought not be too many on the plate. The preacher can attempt to say
one thing and say it very well.

Preachers learn that they should be able to state the theme of their sermon
in a single, clear sentence. Fred Craddock teaches this:

> What is the text saying? In one sentence, and as simply as possible,
> state the message of the text. This should be in one's own words, and
> as an affirmation. . . . At the bottom of a page on which one has scrib-
> bled notes from research and reflection, the preacher will write a sen-
> tence such as: "Every Christian is a charismatic," or, "Hope can survive
> on almost nothing," or "Prayer is a learned experience," or, "The res-
> urrection of Jesus is God's vindication of self-giving love," or "God's
> grace seems unfair because it is impartial." Writing that sentence
> marks a genuine achievement, rewarded not only by a sense of satis-
> faction but by a new appetite for the next task: the sermon itself.[8]

If the primary theological import of the text can be so plainly stated, why don't
preachers simply state their theme sentence and sit down? They continue to

speak, developing the theme because the point of the sermon is not just to make theological claims, but to engage listeners in scriptural stories, images, or themes, and to move them both to understanding and response. Drawing on both functions of language, preaching is an attempt to convey theological information and to move the heart. It is the literal content that can be stated in one sentence. The development of channels of resonance, the creation of worlds real enough to be recognized and entered, the establishment of a transparent domain that discloses Christ—these are the elements of preaching that depend on carefully chosen language, verbal enfleshment, and poetic development.

The development of literal assertions by means of poetic measures is good news for the preacher in a second way. There are times when the literal assertions that the preacher wishes to make are already well known. The kerygmatic message is an old one. It hasn't changed since the Scripture was canonized. A friend who grew up in an unchurched household once came to worship with me on Passion Sunday and heard for the first time the story of Jesus' arrest, trial, and crucifixion. After the service she turned to me, moved and disturbed, and said: "How could they do that to this man?" For her, the story *was* new. But, for most of our listeners there will be some familiarity with the scriptural texts from which we preach. How does one bring new life into a message that is old? How does the preacher tell the story of the gospel anew when it is a story that is widely known? How can a preacher speak with freshness about a passage that has been preached to a congregation numerous times? The good news for the preacher is that there is no requirement that preaching say something new. The gospel speaks for itself in its timeless pertinence to the human condition. The preacher's job is not to speak a new word but *to speak an old word in a new way.* This is the vocation of the artist: to bring the listener to an awareness of something new that is born of the preacher's knowledge of faith and its relation to life. Preaching is like an old stove. It doesn't matter how often it has cradled the gospel's fire. On a cold morning it is still good to draw near to its familiar shape to be warmed again.

Preachers with years of experience will recognize the situation that gives rise to the sermon example that follows. When a pastor or priest preaches in a congregation season after season and year after year, he or she will encounter recurring texts and seasonal themes. For preachers who subscribe to the guidance of the three-year lectionary, certain texts come their way on an annual basis. For example, John 1:1–18 is appointed as the gospel lesson for the second Sunday after Christmas in all three years of the cycle. And, in the rotation of the seasons of the church year, preachers are called on annually to address the significance of the incarnation, aspects of Epiphany, the meaning of Advent or Lent, and the resurrection. Preachers involved in a long-term ministry in a congregation may weary of trying to find yet another profound insight into those texts and themes that have been probed repeatedly. The story is told of a well-known preacher whose Easter sermons were highly anticipated rhetorical events. He stepped into the pulpit one Easter morning and said, "Christ is Risen! Go tell somebody," and then sat down. An alternative approach would be this: In answer to the question, "What is the point I would like to make this time?" the preacher might choose to make no point at all. The preacher might simply choose to let the biblical story speak for itself, but to tell it from a fresh perspective. In this type of preaching, as Richard Jensen says, "the story is the point."[9] What follows is a rendering of the story of the crucifixion, as preached in a congregation where I had preached on Good Friday five consecutive years. The point of the sermon is not to make any theological claims about the meaning of the event, but simply to draw the listeners into a closer view of something already known.

It was a bright spring morning. The usually dry countryside was transformed by recent rain. Hills and ravines, meadows and valleys were covered again with life. Over the landscape lay a thick, green carpet, decorated with the vivid colors of new blossoms: shades of blue and purple, splashes of orange, random yellows, and dashes of white. The birds sang their songs of praise through the morning mist. Newborn lambs bounced playfully in the pastures. A gentle breeze tickled the new leaves on the olive trees and made them shimmer, silver-green, silver-green, silver-green. A few bright clouds slid gently across a distant sky.

It was a day full of life. All creation was newly alive, stretching and growing, breathing and moving, dancing and playing, living and smiling.

But, slowly, it began to change. Just when the sun was high and the mist had burned away, clouds began to form, to gather, to brood, moving in a slow boil. Minute by minute, they rolled and turned, growing darker and more threatening. But there was no sound, no thunder, no lightning to herald a spring rain. Only the quiet, ominous gathering of something dark in the glowering sky. A shadow fell over the faces of the flowers. The air grew cold; the birds and the lambs instinctively prepared themselves for a storm that was not to come.

The clouds troubled themselves for hours until by midday, the sky was close, thick, and dark. As if it were nighttime, not a ray of life-giving sunlight penetrated the velvet canopy that covered the earth. Darkness clung to its surface as time drew a slow, labored breath.

Then, quite suddenly, the earth fell silent. The birds stopped their singing. The sheep looked skyward in mute wonder. The wind stood perfectly still, stirring neither a forest leaf nor a blade of pasture grass. Meadow ponds, without a ripple, became mirrors reflecting the pressing blackness above. Even the sinners grew still for the moment as somewhere, on a lonely hilltop, the Lord of Creation breathed his last few breaths and sighed in death.

Then, just as suddenly there came a deep, anguished, bowel-watering groan from far below. All creation lent its voice to the earth which alone broke the silence. The sound was not loudness but power; more felt than heard, more agonizing than terrible, more anguished than wrathful. Deep within its granite crust the earth convulsed, twisted, grinding stone on stone, squeezing hot lava between fissures, wrenching the planet's skeleton and upheaving its skin. Mountains moved, hills shook, rivers stopped, the ground broke open in crevices and deeply buried tombs spilled forth their contents. The earth moved and mourned the moment the Lord of Creation gave up his life.

Then the earth, grieved and spent, cared like a mother for her Creator. In a garden she opened a womb, a small stony receptacle, and placed him inside.

The sun returned with its warmth the next day and burned away the morning mist. The birds and lambs resumed their play and their praise. The breeze stirred the flowers and leaves. But, in all their activity, there was a different tone, a lingering sense of incompleteness. In all it did, in all it said, from the brook's gentle babble to the eagle's shrill cry, all creation, except for the sinners, prayed that this would not be the end, that somehow, in that small stone-cold womb, springtime would return and life would stir again.

THE PREACHER AS POET

When I was recently having lunch with a professor of homiletics, our discussion turned to the topic of her upcoming research project. Having written significantly on the theology of preaching, she was hoping that this new project might have a more affective component; that her new work might function in the way that preaching works, not just to illuminate the mind but to move the heart. It was an approach that I readily embraced. "Yet," said this homiletician, "I'm not sure I can do it."

"Of course you can," I countered.

"But I'm not a poet."

Whether you view preaching as poetry or not, what is clear is that preaching well involves the poetic use of language. Even if preachers do not write poems, they think and work poetically. If they fail in this, their preaching is mere discourse. The homiletician in the story is a superb wordsmith whose preaching is theologically kerygmatic and aesthetically engaging. She *is* a poet, although she does not write poems. What she writes are sermons, filled with imagery, evocative language, and the identifiable stuff of life. Her sermons create virtual realms that are known by the listener and that are engaging on a deep and personal level.

This preacher's writing skills have been fed by the fruit of feminist theology. One of the gifts that feminism has brought to preaching is a keener focus on the imaginative use of language. Christine M. Smith has conducted a survey among homileticians in the United States and has received comments about the distinctive qualities of women's preaching. A summary of her findings indicates that, compared with typical male preaching, women's preaching tends to be better crafted and delivered, more creative and imaginative in textual analysis, more filled with image and story, more concerned with real-life issues, more inclusive, and more inclined to be directed to the heart rather than to the mind of the listener.[10] "These observations about women's preaching," Smith concludes, "helped me discern key issues in the development of a view of preaching from a feminist perspective."[11]

Smith's observations indicate that feminist preaching is concerned with the use of poetic language in service of the gospel. Her conclusions seem to suggest that, at least in relation to the use of verbal symbols, women tend to resonate more in their sermon construction and delivery with the creative capacity of the Creator. Still earthen vessels, their sermons tend to be more like crystal than clay.

There is a temptation, at this point, to challenge the observations and tendencies of Smith's project. Might one find similar trends in preaching that derive from other theological perspectives? How does womanist preaching (which embraces more of the African American woman's perspective) compare to these conclusions? And does not liberation theology bring unique poetic gifts to the pulpit? One might even argue that much of the preaching of white males (some long dead, others still productive) is highly evocative and imaginative. (My own experience with students has been that the most gifted wordsmiths have been found equally among men and women.) However, the point here is not to debate the uniqueness of the qualities of feminist theology but to embrace the gift it brings to the pulpit. If feminist preaching tends to be more imaginative, more poetic than other preaching, then we can thank the movement for raising the possibility of affective sensitivity and aesthetic responsivity in the pulpit. If Smith's conclusions are sound, there is something to be learned from feminist preaching by all who would preach in ways that touch people deeply and move the heart. The gift of feminist theology is a gift not just to women preachers but to all preachers. More important, it is a gift to the church, to all who will listen to and be touched by sermons that are crafted with poetic care.

If the preacher is a poet, then a question of aesthetic theory arises: Are poets (and preachers) born with the creative genius or can they learn the craft? Let's consider the question from two perspectives. The first is philosophical.

Reynolds Price, the award-winning and prolific poet, playwright, and novelist, discovered two things in his own growth as a writer. First,

> the writer of durable fiction, poetry, and drama arises from gifts that resemble the gift of sanctity and cannot be taught. The skills required are genetic or at least intrinsic endowments that cannot be willfully coaxed to life and then fanned into a lasting and manageable flame.[12]

The key to this statement is the term "durable." Because preaching is an event that is prophetic—that is, it speaks God's Word for a particular moment and a particular people—it does not need to be durable. It does need to be pertinent and to be filled with promise and presence. The power of preaching comes primarily in its ability to address the needs and concerns of the people for whom it is written and to whom it is delivered. There are devotional and instructional reasons for sermons to be published, read, and studied. Yet sermons are successful primarily in their ability to serve as vehicles to disclose the Divine Presence and promise in intimate and immediate circumstances, such as the worshiping assembly of believers. If sermons have an afterlife, if they are durable, they exceed their primary purpose. For preachers who seek to write durable sermons, Price's observation stands as a warning. Not everyone will have the genius to do so.

The second of Price's observations about the craft of language use is more encouraging for preachers and would-be poets:

> Imaginative writing—like painting, sculpture, musical composition, dancing, singing, and the playing of instruments—can be taught like mathematics and the tango to gifted and disciplined students. The history, since Greece and Rome, of instruction in rhetoric, music, and the fine arts (especially painting) provides unanswerable proof of the success of such instruction when intelligently offered and diligently received.[13]

Here, the preacher and poet are heartened. Not only can the basic skills of preaching be taught (exegesis, hermeneutics, theological exposition, rhetoric, and delivery), but the particulars of poetic writing can be taught and learned by diligent and disciplined students. Peter Elbow, another writer and teacher of writing, concurs. Elbow speaks about the value of engaging in exercises in metaphorical thinking. "If you use them regularly," he says, "you will gradually increase your creative and imaginative capacity."[14] He goes on to disagree with Aristotle, who said rightly that the use of metaphor is the mark of human intelligence, but was wrong "when he said that it could not be learned."[15] What Christine Smith teaches from the feminist perspective is something that all preachers can learn. We can turn cold homiletical discourse into vigorous preaching, or what Jana Childers calls a "lively homiletic,"[16] through the use of nondiscursive or presentational language. By means of such language, our sermons become richer in human insight and able more deeply to quarry the veins and deposits of human experience.

The second perspective from which to answer the question of learning to preach with poetic imagination is a theological one. In a certain sense, all believers are involved in proclamation. They tell their own stories of faith both discursively, in their conversations with others, and in the way that they live their lives. People's service and devotion, or their lack, are plain-speaking elements of proclamation. Not all believers, however, are called to be or gifted for the specific ministry of preaching. The sense of being called to particular ministries grows out of Paul's image of the Body of Christ:

> For as in one body we have many members, and not all the members have the same function, so we, who are many, are one body in Christ, and individually we are members one of another. We have gifts that differ according to the grace given to us: prophecy, in proportion to faith; ministry, in ministering; the teacher, in teaching; the exhorter, in exhortation; the giver, in generosity; the leader, in diligence; the compassionate, in cheerfulness. (Rom. 12:4–8)

Paul did not here, and does not elsewhere, claim the status of spiritual gift for preaching. Yet the sense of spiritual call and gift is clearly implied in his work: "For this gospel I was appointed a herald [κῆρυξ; RSV: preacher] and an apostle and a teacher, and for this reason I suffer as I do" (2 Tim. 1:11–12).

The sense of a particular call to preaching is a development of the medieval church. Calvin believed that the call to preach was an external call, different from the more general internal call to hear the Word through the work of the Holy Spirit.[17] John Mulder has traced the history of the call to preach from its medieval inception. He concludes:

> The Protestant movement has also stressed the call to preach. This emphasis has been characteristic of all branches of Protestantism, but it has been particularly strong in African-American churches and Pentecostal and charismatic denominations. The preacher is called by God to proclaim the gospel. That call is a compelling, urgent summons. The preacher must speak because God has provided a message. There is no other choice. As Martin Luther King, Sr., said of his famous son, "The boy was called to preach. He had to, he could do no other."[18]

The Protestant sense of the call, as indicated here, suggests that kerygmatic proclamation is a task that is undertaken by those who have been given the grace to do so. As we have seen, Karl Barth feels strongly about the place of the Holy Spirit in preaching. It is that which makes our attempts at proclamation effective. He also stresses that the Holy Spirit is active in the training of preachers. Preachers must not rely simply on the Holy Spirit, Barth says, but strive with all seriousness to interpret the Word correctly even though recognizing that *recte docere* (correct teaching) can become a reality only by the Holy Spirit. It is for this reason that the church cannot responsibly grant anyone the right to proclaim the Word without a theological education. . . . [T]he true *didaskolos* (teacher) has to be taught by the Holy Spirit. . . .[19]

To summarize these theological assertions, we can say that preaching is a spiritual calling and that the preacher can be taught the skills with which to proclaim God's Word. Just as the Spirit is the source of the call, the Spirit is also the inspiration for the education of the preacher. Because, as we have seen, preaching is an art and the skills of artists can be taught and learned by diligent students, the arts of language use can be learned as well. The formation of the preacher as a poet can be seen, then, as a furthering of grace to preachers who wish to find words to express the Word and to congregations who wish to see Jesus. "But I'm not a poet," we may be tempted to say. The response to this is, once again, gift. God supplies preachers with the grace they need. In learning to preach and striving to preach well, if we attend to the matters of language use, we can trust that in our weakness, the Holy Spirit will intercede for us and bless our learning and our proclamation.

THE POET'S TOOL BAG

What then, can preachers learn from the poets? What tools can we borrow— or better yet, take and keep—from the poet's tool bag? Wordcraft is like woodcraft. All craftsmen and -women have their bags of favorite tools. The more experienced the worker, the more worn and responsive are the tools to the touch. Apprentices' tools are new and coarse, not yet broken in. Masters' tools are the ones to examine: polished here by the wear of the hand, mirrored there by the caress of the wood, rusting in places from the sweat of the master. It is instructive for the learner to look occasionally into the master's bag and see what tools are used and to watch how they are put to work.

There are masterful preachers to learn from, and many have written of their language tools. For learning how homileticians use poetic tools, the reader can consult the following works: Thomas Long addresses the use of three figures of speech in *The Witness of Preaching*: simile, metaphor, and synecdoche. In *Imagery for Preaching*, Patricia Wilson-Kastner develops the concept of imagination in preaching and demonstrates how the use of biblical and life images enables preaching to address the whole person. Ruth Duck teaches about preaching and worship and writes hymns. In *Finding Words for Worship*, she shares her eight-step creative process and demonstrates how it can help preachers engage their imaginations and get their words to flow.[20] Charles Bartow writes about words in *The Preaching Moment: A Guide to Sermon Delivery*. He teaches preachers to speak imagistic words with color and to use images that excite the sound, sight, olfactory, gustatory, tactile, visceral, and kinesthetic senses of the listeners. Another homiletician, Jana Childers, writes about the relationship between preaching and theater. In *Performing the Word: Preaching as Theater*, Childers does not address issues of poetic language construction but gives vivid examples of imaginative writing in her prose. One can learn poetic technique from her simply by reading her text:

> . . . it is worth noting that when questions about what is missing in contemporary preaching are put to laypeople, they yield an age-old and surprisingly consistent response: passion. Call it passion, life, authenticity, naturalness, conviction, sincerity, or being animated. Call it fire, sparks, electricity, mojo, spiritual lava, or juice. It is what listeners want in a preacher. . . . What is it that makes a sermon work, fly, come to life, have zing, take wing, tear the place up? What gets a sermon up off the page, across the tops of the pews, and down into people's insides? What gives preaching transconscious appeal—the kind of impact that affects not just cerebrum but cerebellum too? What is the difference between that kind of sermon and the one that seems to dribble down the front of the pulpit and out into the aisles?[21]

There are others who write helpfully about language use from a theological perspective, writers whose bread and butter is not primarily poetics but homiletics or liturgics.[22]

There are also masters of wordcraft who do not preach, at least not in the kerygmatic sense. For the preacher who wishes to speak engagingly and with power, much can be learned from those who practice an art that is closely parallel to preaching. Our method for the remainder of this chapter will be to look carefully into the tool bags of people who pay their rent by writing well and teaching others their craft. We will not only look at their tools but also take them in hand and feel their weight against the wood through the examples and exercises that are included. The masters who will guide us into this language workshop are: James Kilpatrick, author of *The Writer's Art*; Peter Elbow, whose methods are demonstrated in *Writing with Power: Techniques for Mastering the Writing Process*; Kim Addonizio and Dorianne Laux, coauthors of *The Poet's Companion: A Guide to the Pleasures of Writing Poetry*; and Arthur Quinn, whose wit makes a dry and technical topic come alive in *Figures of Speech: 60 Ways to Turn a Phrase*. As we proceed into the workshop, we will examine several different kinds of tools. Some have to do with the writer's approach, some with poetic devices and figures of speech, others with the completion of the writing task.

THE WRITER'S APPROACH

The first tool of the poet is *perception*. Before poets or preachers pick up a pen or sit down at a keyboard to write, they open their eyes. Before doing anything else, including research, selecting and exegeting a text, or finding a topic to address, they look at the world around them; store the sights, scenes, feelings, tastes, sounds, and smells in the libraries of their experience; and check them out as resources for their writing and speaking. Preachers and poets, like all artists, have a unique way of looking at the world.

Sam Abell is a photographer whose recent work has been published in the National Geographic Society volume, *Lewis and Clark: Voyage of Discovery*. In an interview about this collection of photographs on National Public Radio, he was asked about one picture in particular. It is a photograph of an American bison's eye from the distance of eight inches. How did he get so close to such a large wild beast, the interviewer inquired? Apbel answered that he and a farmer had been feeding cake to a herd of the animals from the back of a pickup truck. When a piece of cake fell to the ground, one of the bison found it and began to nibble on it. Abell quickly crawled under the truck and, from the safety of its cover, was able to inch near the beast until they were, as he said, "literally eye to eye." In commenting on the moment, Abell remarked that as a photographer, it is his job to observe things, to go to unusual places, and to let others see what he sees. Not many people can crawl under a truck to get a close-up of a bison's eye. "That's my job," he said, to crawl under there and "bring that shot home."[23]

The preacher's eye is a camera. It draws in the light and color of the world, captures the contrasts in its scenes and images, highlights areas of shadow and sunshine, and preserves the images for later consideration. When listeners are shown the pictures that are apprehended through the preacher's photographic perspective, they know that they are seeing something real about life, something genuine in nature or in the nature of human relationship.

What the observant preacher captures is more than visual images. Poetic perception involves all the senses. Addonizio and Laux provide guidance here:

> Poets need to keep all five senses—and possibly a few more—on continual alert, ready to translate the world through their bodies, to reinvent it in language. . . . You take a walk outside after the first snowfall of the season, fill your eyes with the dazzling surfaces of the fields and your lungs with the sharp pure air. Your boots sink in, crunching down to the frozen earth, and when you return to the cabin the warmth feels like a pair of gloved hands placed on your cold ears. You sit down and write about the snow. Miles away and years later, someone—a reader—closes her eyes and experiences it.[24]

Kilpatrick describes perception as the first secret of good writing: "We must look *intently*, and hear *intently*, and taste *intently*. . . . we must look at everything very hard."[25] When Addonizio and Laux looked at snow, they saw "dazzling white." Kilpatrick looks harder:

> Is the task to describe a snowfall? Very well, we begin by observing that the snow is white. Is it as white as bond paper? White as whipped cream? Is the snow daisy white, or eggwhite white, or whitewash white? Let us look very hard. We will see that snow comes in different textures. The light snow that looks like powdered sugar is not the heavy snow that clings like wet cotton. When we write matter-of-factly that *Last night it snowed and this morning the fields were white*, we haven't said much. We have not looked *intently*.[26]

Seeing with all your senses is the first step. Finding a way to record them is the next. This involves *selection*. From chapter 1 on, I have made reference to a particular phrase that was coined by philosopher Susanne Langer. She says that the artist selects from the symbols at hand those which, according to the "logical rightness and necessity of expression," will yield the best presentation of an artist's ideas. Ideas can be expressed in many ways; some are more accurate and appropriate than others. Selecting symbols or words according to the rightness and necessity of expression allows for artists to "say what they mean and not something else."[27] For artists whose symbols are words, such as preachers and poets, there are three challenges. The first is to select those words that give an accurate account of what is meant. We are constantly looking not just for words, but for the right words. We seek, as Mark Twain observed, "to use the right word, and not its second cousin."[28] Kilpatrick shows us what Twain means: "When we read that a 'house has been robbed,' we are meeting a second cousin, for houses are burglarized; people are robbed."[29] "A powerful agent is the right word," Twain says:

> it lights the reader's way and makes it plain; a close approximation to it will answer, and much traveling is done in a well-enough fashion by its help, but we do not welcome it and applaud it and rejoice in it as we do when the right one blazes out on us. . . . One has no time to examine the [right] word and vote upon its rank and standing, the automatic recognition of its supremacy is so immediate. There is a plenty of acceptable literature which deals largely in approximations, but it may be likened to a fine landscape seen through the rain; the right word would dismiss the rain, then you would see it better.[30]

Or, to put in terms we have used previously, for preachers to serve as Philip so that the people may see Jesus, learning to use the right words enables the Presence and the promise to be more clearly disclosed and the preacher to be more hidden.

The second challenge in selection is to find words that are evocative, that appeal to the senses, that perform a bit of magic in us. As Addonizio and Laux show us, words that create sensory images work like this: when we encounter the image of a lighted cigarette or a glass of wine being poured,

> the scent of smoke or grapes is in the air. Some synapse in your brain has been nudged and produces the memory of the aroma. Magic. That's what an image should do, produce a bit of magic, a reality so real it is "like being alive twice."[31]

A third challenge in selection, as Kilpatrick reminds us, is to select not just the exact word or the vivid word. It must also be the appropriate word. "We ought to keep a steady eye on the audience we are addressing. Slang has its place; idiom has its place; the easygoing colloquialism has its place, and even profanity has its place, but their places are not always the same places."[32] In a beginning preaching class, a student preacher admonished his listeners by paraphrasing a familiar maxim: "We must defecate or get off the pot." It is not difficult to imagine sermon settings where such a statement would pass the pale of good taste.

Perception and selection are two keys to the writer's approach. They can be practiced by preachers who would both convey information to their hearers and move them to response and transformation. The following exercises are offered as a means to practice elements of the writer's approach. They are similar to those other artists use,[33] for it is the job of all artists to give expression to elements of human experience that are too deep for words.

Exercises in Perception and Selection

1. Take a snapshot of a colorful scene with your eyes, taking in hues, shades, depths. Return to your memory of it the next day and describe what you saw. Try to find words that describe both accurately and vividly the colors and shapes of your remembered image.

   EXAMPLES[34]

   Regarding a walk in an autumn forest: Near me stood a maple tree that had, perhaps a night or two before, exploded. But the burst was flash-frozen, caught in the precise instant of its greatest energy and crimson brilliance. Everywhere around me were images of fire: trees and bushes caught in various stages of frozen combustion.

   The desert was a hot, dry, dun-colored plain; a thousand square miles of medium-grit sandpaper.

2. Observe an ordinary event, focusing not on how it looks but how it is perceived by another sense or how it feels. (Closing your eyes may help you focus.) Concentrate on the range of sensation that is perceived. Write down your observations, trying to describe the fullness of the experience.

EXAMPLES

The forest symphony was loosely orchestrated. The main motif was a sparrow solo, fluted repeatedly. In layers of counterpoint, other voices could be heard: here and there clarinets called antiphonally; an occasional viola fiddling a trill and the high harmonic cricket violin; a persistent piccolo called from offstage; high overhead an oboe circled, its reedy voice faintly distinct; and behind them all, the soft tapping of the snare as the brittle leaves fell in crisp piles.

Fear is a small cell with no air in it and no light. It is suffocating inside, and dark. There is no room to turn around inside it. You can only face in one direction, but it hardly matters since you cannot see anyhow. There is no future in the dark. Everything is over. Everything is past. When you are locked up like that, tomorrow is as far away as the moon.[35]

Barbara Brown Taylor

3. Describe an object or an action as if to someone who cannot see it. Try to capture the character of its appearance using words that don't relate to sight.

EXAMPLES

If you're not familiar with the trillium, imagine the flower that would come from a flute if a flute could make a flower. That is the trillium, a work of God from a theme by Mozart.[36]

James Kilpatrick

. . . the sound of sunlight can be deafening at noon.[37]

Barbara Brown Taylor

Ivar's gaze landed on Nils with an almost perceptible thud.[38]

Jane Smiley

FIGURES OF SPEECH

Figures are the writer's hammer and saw: indispensable. They are also known as tropes or turns of phrase. There are many of them, and scholars have undertaken to categorize them and determine how some turns, though similar, are different from others and how some figures are subsets of larger categories. For example, a *zeugma* is the ellipsis of a verb from one of two parallel clauses ("Out of Zion shall go forth instruction, and the word of the LORD from Jerusalem," Isa. 2:3), but a *hypozeuxis* occurs, says Arthur Quinn, "when you could have used a zeugma but didn't."[39] Of course, preachers don't need to know much about the technical names of figures of speech. Quinn gives the names of sixty figures in his book "only to show that I am systematizing customary distinctions. I would expect no one," he admits, "except a fool or a scholar, to want to learn them—and perhaps not even the fool."[40] We don't need to know their names in order to employ figures. But their use is, as I said, indispensable to good writing and good preaching.

> Writing is not chemical engineering. We shouldn't learn the figures of speech the way we learn the periodic table of elements. We shouldn't because we are learning not about hypothetical structures in things, but about real potentialities within our language, within ourselves.[41]

Figures of speech enable us to employ the plasticity of language. We figure the language in unusual ways, using one image to mean another, breaking the rules of grammar for effect, placing things in odd juxtapositions. Through these twists and turns (and many more) we are able to say things with depth, clarity, insight, surprise, and truth. It is due to the turnability of language that we can think of expressing things that are too deep for ordinary words. We figure the language, presenting new facets of understanding and complex levels of meaning that resonate with others who feel similar things and have shared experiences but do not know how to speak of them. When a listener encounters an apt metaphor in a sermon or Scripture, it might be just that odd juxtaposition of contrary ideas that speaks to the sharply felt mysteries of life and faith. Jesus is Living Water, for example, slaking a thirst that is felt more unfathomably than the throat-deep parchedness of a dehydrated body.

There are many kinds of figures, more than most writers or speakers would try to use. But there are some that will be useful to preachers who wish to freshen their language and use it to probe more deeply the levels of human sentience. Here are definitions and examples of a number of useful figures of speech:

The *enallage* is a figure that is employed when a writer or speaker breaks a grammatical rule. The most famous enallage, perhaps, comes from Joe Jacobs, a prizefight manager who, in 1932, commented on the decision against his fighter: "We was robbed!" It sounds like a grammatical error by one who might not know better. But it has the force of anger, frustration, and disappointment. "If he had said 'were'," explains Quinn, "he likely would have been consigned to the same oblivion as was the smug winning manager."[42] Using an enallage enables the writer to say something with peculiar and memorable effectiveness—thus, *Punch* magazine's "You pays your money, you takes your choice," or James Joyce's Molly Brown, who says, "My patience are exhausted."[43] Or in a sermon, you might hear "If you ain't got Jesus, you ain't got nothin'." We know it is crude, unattractive, almost vulgar speech. It's all wrong, and yet in the proper place it is just right.

When you choose to use too many conjunctions, you are using a *polysyndeton*. Placing an "and" between items in a list can give the sense that each item is of equal importance: "You shall love the Lord your God with all your heart, and with all our soul, and with all your strength, and with all your mind; and your neighbor as yourself" (Luke 10:27). A polysyndeton can also suggest that the items listed are in order of growing importance: "She was a doctor, and a teacher, and a woman, and a daughter, and a mother." Or it can suggest that a temporal relationship exists between the listed items: "When men drink, then they are rich and successful and win lawsuits and are happy and help their friends. Quickly, bring me a beaker of wine" (Aristophanes).[44]

Doing the opposite, omitting an expected conjunction, is to employ an *asyndeton*. Its use is quite common. Lincoln concluded his address at Gettysburg with one: "That government of the people, by the people, for the people, shall not perish from the earth." If you use an asyndeton, you will find yourself in good company, not only Lincoln, but Jesus (or at least, Mark): "For it is from within, from the human heart, that evil intentions come: fornication, theft, murder, adultery, avarice, wickedness, deceit, licentiousness, envy, slander, pride, folly. All these things come from within, and they defile a person" (Mark 7:21–23). And Paul: "And now faith, hope, love abide, these three; and the greatest of these is love" (1 Cor. 13:13). Using an asyndeton quickens your phrase, giving it a sense of immediacy. It also gives the sense that the items listed are bound in close relationship.

Sometimes you might wish to omit more than a conjunction. You might wish to punctuate your prose by using a *sentence fragment*. They are used commonly in our conversational speech. Some writers suggest, however, that it is inappropriate in more formal prose. Kilpatrick disagrees, in an exemplary fashion:

> They mistakenly suppose that the rules of grammar forbid the *sentence fragment*. Humbug. Nonsense. No Way. Our purpose in writing is to convey thought. No rule says that thought *always* must be conveyed on the parlor cars of a proper subject and a proper predicate. There are times, especially when you have subjected your readers to a string of long and complex sentences, sorely taxing their concentration, when a sentence fragment comes as a welcome relief. No fooling.[45]

Some things bear repeating. *Repetition* comes in many forms—accumulatio, diacope, and symploce, to name a few. The power of repetition is in its insistence. Like the request of the importuning widow of Luke 18, repeated words, phrases, and structures strike our ears and hammer our perceptions until we cannot escape their persistent message. Repetition is an effective and often used element of writing and speech. Martin Luther King Jr. used it masterfully. Gertrude Stein was famous for it: "Rose is a rose is a rose is a rose."[46] Kilpatrick remarks that it is the quality of repetition that marks great oratory:

> Over a long lifetime, I have wondered, how many speeches will a reporter hear? The mind boggles. In person, on the tube, or on

recordings, a journalist will listen to thousands. Only a handful are truly memorable, and in each of them, we hear the device of repetition.[47]

He cites Churchill's famous speech at the onset of war as an example: "We shall fight on the seas and oceans . . . we shall fight on the beaches, we shall fight on the landing grounds, we shall fight in the fields and in the streets, we shall fight in the hills; we shall never surrender."[48]

The purpose of repetition is to give rhetorical shape to discourse and to keep the audience near the center of the writer's message. This can be accomplished in many ways. Churchill has used *anaphora*, the repetition of words at the beginnings of phrases or sentences. It is common in preaching. John Donne provides an example:

> Here, in the prayers of the Congregation God comes to us; here, in his Ordinance of Preaching, God delivers himselfe to us; here in the administration of his Sacraments, he seals, ratifies, confirmes all unto us.[49]

Another technique is called *repetend*, the irregular repetition of a word, phrase, or image throughout a discourse. Anne Page has consented to the use of this example from a sermon on John the Baptist. She introduces the figure vividly, describing his unusual clothing, wild appearance, his filth, and concludes that he is like "the relative that no one talks about at Thanksgiving." She keeps us near this wild, frightening, embarrassing figure throughout the sermon by interjecting his image and voice: "John nods his head . . . 'Good,' he says." Again, "John shakes his head in pity . . . 'No, no.'" Later, "'Get in the river,' John says." And finally, "'Ah,' John nods his head. 'You are starting to get it.'"

Sometimes the use of repetition will determine the sermon's form. Like some psalms and hymns, the sermon might be structured around a *refrain*. It might take the shape of the poetry of the first chapter of Genesis, where a succession of comments are united by the recurring "And there was evening and there was morning, the first (second, third, etc.) day." A sermon might also follow the shape of a musical form of repetition known as *recapitulation*. In this, a theme is stated (A), is developed (B), and is stated again or recapitulated (A). One finds the ABA form in sermons that begin with a story or image as a way to introduce the sermon topic, then develop the theme in the body of the sermon, and bring closure by returning in the conclusion to the opening scene or image.

Some forms of repetition are disguised. *Antithesis*, for example, is repetition by negation. "Rather than saying something and then repeating it in other words, you both deny its contrary and assert it."[50] It is an alternative to simple repetition and has the benefit of lending a definitive thrust to an assertion.

"All things came into being through him, and without him not one thing came into being" (John 1:3).

Another figure whose power lies in its negative association is *oxymoron*. This is a pair or combination of words that are contradictory or incongruous. The word comes from the Greek and means *pointedly foolish*. Its use adds a touch of irony to a description. Kilpatrick offers some tantalizing samples: a professor on leave whose title is "professor in residence in absentia," "efficient bureaucracy," and a hastily done hairdo by a famous stylist who described it as "elegant messy."[51]

Some figures of speech derive not from negative association but from partial association. *Metonymy* is one. This is making reference to an object or condition by substituting a lesser, related one. When people in news media use "the White House" to refer to the President or the presidency, they are using metonymy. The psalms are rich with examples. "Save me, O God, by your name" (Ps. 54:1) uses "name" to imply God's strength and power over adversaries. "Awake, O harp and lyre" (Ps. 108:2) is not a call to inanimate objects but to the person who plays them. Metonymy is a form of understatement. It denotes more than it says.[52] Closely related to metonymy is *synecdoche*. (Quinn categorizes synecdoche as a subclass of metonymy.) In this figure, a part of an object is used to stand for the whole. The common example is the use of the word "heart" to refer to the whole person: "Yet, poor old heart, he holp the heavens to rain" (King Lear). The power of the synecdoche comes from the association that is made between the characteristic of the part that is implied in the whole. "My beloved is mine and I am his; he pastures his flock among the lilies" (Song 2:16). In this example, "lilies" represents the pastures of spring, and the beauty of the flowers is implied in the larger part. A coarser example demonstrates the principle at work in a negative way. "Get your tail over here" implies that the one who is being summoned is as unrespectable as that person's hindmost part.

Among the more commonly used figures of speech are *simile* and *metaphor*. Some figures of these types are so often employed in everyday speech, in fact, that they lose their power to enliven our language or help us to see things from new perspectives.

> The trouble is that most of the figures in our language are so common and have been heard so often that they're virtually useless for poetry, which deals not in clichéd, worn-out expressions but in surprising ones that reveal new connections or cast a different angle of light on an idea or experience.[53]

Effective similes and metaphors place things in odd juxtapositions, leading, and sometimes forcing, readers and hearers to consider connections between them. They help us to deepen or expand our understanding of things by virtue of the unexpected comparison. Hackneyed figures lose the sense of surprise and place things and ideas in anticipated comparisons.

A simile is the comparison of one thing with another, with the suggestion that the one is in a singular way like the other. "Good similes," quips Kilpatrick, "can light up a paragraph as a smile lights up a face."[54] They may, though do not necessarily, use the words "as," "like," or "is similar to" in order to draw the comparison: "Preaching is *like* an old stove" or "The singer's vibrato oscillated with the speed and punctuation of a machine gun." The power of the simile is in its ability to demonstrate some quality in an unknown or not fully understood entity by linking it to another that is known. When Kilpatrick was reporting on a racketeering trial, he described a repulsive, green-suited, Fifth Amendment–spouting witness in terms that anyone could know: he was "like a frog on a lily pad, dripping hostility from hooded eyes, and repeatedly croaking 'duh privilege.'"[55] Similes also strengthen expression because they can be brief and direct. Here are two examples, striking, though not ones you would use in a sermon. From Norman Dubie's poem "The Funeral": "The cancer ate her like horse piss eats deep snow."[56] And from Reynolds Price's journals: "Martha Reynolds said the first weekend he flew Mildred down to Inez, they landed in Gid's pasture and it scared the old cow so bad that every tit sat out like a pot leg and squirted milk."[57]

Metaphors are like similes in that they bring into comparison things that aren't usually associated. "Every metaphor is a force-fit, a mistake, a putting together of things that don't normally or literally belong together."[58] Metaphor is stronger than simile in that it does not suggest a comparison but insists on it. One thing is not merely like something else; it *is* something else. Whereas simile leads a listener to a comparison, metaphor forces the comparison on the listener's perception. The writer of John's Gospel knew the force of metaphor and tells us that Jesus is not merely like a lamb being led to slaughter; he is the Lamb of God. Thus, the bloody images of the slaughterhouse are forced into our consideration of God's sacrifice in the crucifixion of Jesus.

Metaphors can be brief and make a quick point: "Metaphors are the icing on the pound cake of ordinary prose," and "a touch of brandy in the sauce of style."[59] They can also be extended. Both poems and sermons can be cast in the frame of extended metaphor. To preach a sermon on God as Parent or Judge or Mother Hen would be to sustain it on the image of something that God is obviously not, yet, upon reflection, rather is.

For metaphor to have its greatest effect, it needs to be fresh. Kilpatrick describes a number of circumstances where writers tried for apt expression but failed because their metaphors were stale. "In these instances, the metaphors collapsed from the weight of the clichés in which they were fashioned: *stranglehold, logjams, launching pads, cold shoulders, back burners,* and *holding patterns.*"[60] The solution, he says, is "to make them like breakfast biscuits, fresh every morning."[61] Fresh metaphors for preachers can grow out of one's biblical study. The Scriptures are rich with images that have not been so overused as to fall limply on the imagination. Some pericopes offer internal images that can be used in preaching to sustain homiletical development. The psalms alone are a rich resource. In addition to well-known images, such as God as a rock, refuge, eagle, king, and shadow, there are others that can be employed with fresh effect. They include "wagon tracks" overflowing with richness, God catching us in a "net," enemies as "smoke" to be driven away, and songs of praise that "ride" upon the clouds.

The importance of metaphor for preaching has been stated most clearly by David Buttrick. As preachers, we have the responsibility to speak in ways that address things too deep for words. For Buttrick, there is only one way to do this: "The only way we have access to our own depth is by metaphor."[62] Metaphoric language is so appropriate to preaching that Buttrick says categorically, "Preaching mediates metaphorically."[63]

Exercises in Crafting Figures of Speech

Not all figures of speech will require practice in order to employ them. Enallage, for example, may come all too easily to some speakers. Methods of repetition or the addition or deletion of conjunctions can be adapted readily. They are like the hammer. If you see one at work in another's hands, you immediately sense how you would use it. The exercises that follow allow the preacher to take in hand three tools that require more practice to use well: metonymy, synecdoche, and metaphor.

1. Metonymy: Consider an entity, concept, or condition. Make a list of less important objects or circumstances that are closely associated with it. Mark the qualities that might be implied if the related object were used as a substitute for the original.

   EXAMPLES

   Person: a police officer
   Associations and Implications:
       the badge: civic authority, protection
       the uniform: identifiability, commonness of purpose
       the gun: power, violence, defense
       handcuffs: custody, loss of freedom

Concept: Socialism
Associations and Implications:
    uniformity: lack of choice, equality of opportunity, indoctrination
    commune: opportunity for employment, forced labor
    military forces: defense, promulgation of doctrine
    utilitarianism: lack of creativity, simplicity, effectiveness

Condition: being hospitalized
Associations and Implications:
    intravenous tubes: immobility, loss of independence
    hospital bed: weakness, discomfort
    bedpan: humiliation, lack of privacy
    television: lack of purpose, time wasted

2. Synecdoche: Craft a sentence that makes reference to a person or an object. Identify his, her, or its constituent parts. Substitute the parts for the whole and note the possible implications that accrue to the sentence as a result of the substitution.

EXAMPLES

From high atop a windswept hill, the *church* cast its shadow on the community below.
From high atop a windswept hill, the *steeple* cast its shadow . . . (implying the church's transcendence over human circumstances).
From high atop a windswept hill, the *pulpit* cast its shadow . . . (suggesting the power of God's Word over the lives of the people).
From high atop a windswept hill, the *font* (or the *altar*) cast its shadow . . . (implying the importance of the sacraments in the life of the community).

3. Metaphor: Design questions that force you to think in abstract terms about the thing you wish to describe. Form the questions by thinking in categories that are not related to your object. The questions may not yield metaphors that can be used as they are, but they prime the pump for creating fresh images.

EXAMPLES

Of the 48 colors in a box of crayons, which is the color of justice?
What is the sound that knowledge makes?
What food describes the way a person moved?
Which musical term best suggests the smell of a hayloft?
At what time of day does Jane occur?
Toward which geographical directions do pride and humility point?
If serving the poor were a sonata, who would be its composer?
What color would a tiger's stripes be if the tiger were fear?
How would it feel to put on a coat that was forgiveness?
Who would still be breathing if the air were suddenly fire?
How would you describe the taste of wine using adjectives relating to sculpture?
If peace were a bomb, how would it explode?

POETIC DEVICES

Drawing distinctions between figures of speech and poetic devices seems to be a tricky business. Some writers group them all together and speak of them interchangeably. Kilpatrick counts simile, metaphor, alliteration, antithesis, and sentence fragment simply as writer's tools.[64] Hymn writer Austin Lovelace writes of poetic devices as including metaphors, rhetorical devices, figures of speech, and forms of repetition.[65] For our purposes here, let me distinguish between them in this way. Figures of speech are ways of turning the language and using it to surprise and deepen understanding. Poetic devices have a narrower purpose. They are techniques that make our verbal expression come alive through sound. In a sense, they are musical devices, dealing with the way that words sing, fall on the ear, and strike us emotionally. There are a number of such devices that will aid the preacher. They include euphony, alliteration, assonance, consonance, onomatopoeia, rhyme, rhythm, and meter.

Euphony refers to the pleasantness of sound that can occur when words and phrases are spoken. The judgment regarding pleasant sounds is always a matter of personal taste. Several years ago, I used the word "envisagement" in my doctoral thesis. When one of my readers returned a draft to me for revisions, he had scribbled in the margin, "This is an ugly word." Ugly words might be used in preaching for effect. Beautiful words and phrases can also be used to good effect. Martin Luther King Jr. "delighted in euphony," says Richard Lischer:

> it was a pleasure for him to lament the plight of black Americans in
> three rhymed phrases of equal syllabic length:
>   humiliating oppression,
>   the ungodly exploitation,
>   the crushing domination.[66]

There are many ways to say things. The principle of euphony can guide you to search for the right words that allow you to express yourself with both precision and beauty.

One way to craft pleasant-sounding language is to use *alliteration* and *assonance*. Alliteration is the repetition of consonant sounds in a phrase. The repeated sounds can fall at the beginning of words, as in "hostility from hooded eyes." Another, subtler pattern is to place the consonance inside a word: "euphonic felicity." Regarding the use of alliteration, Kilpatrick offers a helpful caution: "It must be used with extreme care. If we put it purposely to work in every paragraph . . . we probably will not prompt our patient readers into palpably protracted panegyrics."[67]

Assonance is the use of repeated vowel sounds in a phrase. It creates a pleasant, though subtle, sound of rhyme within a phrase, as in this example by

Reynolds Price from the poem "Jesus": "I said as much to test their edge/ And
waited for the question. . . ."[68] In this instance, the "eh" sound occurs four
times and builds a sense of aural cohesion in the phrase. Assonance can also
repeat sounds that are near or slant rhymes: "And all will have happy hearts."
In addition to the favorable effect of internal rhyme, assonance allows a sentence to sing. Singers learn that it is the vowel that sustains the musical line
in a text. Only a few consonants, such as *l, m, n, r, w,* and *v,* can be made with
vocalization and pitch. The production of the other consonant sounds
requires vocalization to cease momentarily. (For a full discussion of this phe-
nomenon, see the material on vocal production in chapter 7.) For this reason,
singers rely on the vowels in a text to elongate the musical sound and create
smooth, seamless phrasing. Vowels also allow singers to broaden their tones
with resonance. In crafting texts that will be spoken, the writer can select
words with assonant sounds that will phrase smoothly and allow for resonant
projection.

When the opposite effect is desired, a writer can select words rich with crisp
consonants. Not surprisingly, this poetic device is called *consonance.* The use of
strong consonants can break up a sentence's phrasing and punctuate it with
small percussions. Coupled with the use of short phrases, this might be an
effect a preacher would use to bring a burst of energy or describe a catastrophic
event: "Mountains moved, hills shook, rivers stopped, the ground broke
open in crevices, and deeply buried tombs spilled forth their contents."

Similar effects can be achieved by employing *onomatopoeia,* the use of words
that sound like what they refer to. Bells *jangle,* doors *bang,* cows *moo,* and skirts
swish. With regard to its use, Kilpatrick offers two helpful cautions. The first
echoes his advice regarding alliteration: "the occasions for its use are few."[69] His
second caveat reminds us of the first rule of the writer's approach: perception.

> Listen *intently,* and do not fake it. Sometimes an axe, cutting into a
> tree, goes *thud*; sometimes it goes *whack*; it depends upon the sharp-
> ness of the axe, the kind of tree being cut, the skill of the woodsman,
> and the heaviness of the air. In our house we have two wind-up clocks.
> One goes *plink,* the other goes *bong.* If our purpose is to transcribe
> sound, or to evoke the memory of sound, let us go at the task with
> care—but let us try.[70]

Sometimes the preacher may wish to use *rhyme* more boldly than as in the
use of assonance. This can be incorporated into prose not simply by quoting
from poems and hymns. Rhymes can be woven into a text to heighten the
intensity of expression, create a memorable summation, or bring a quality of
repose to one's words. The rhyme can be situated within a phrase (internal
rhyme): "The blade was made of finest steel." Or it can be placed, as in most

hymns, at the end of lines. Here is an example from a preaching student, Stephen Faller. In this instance, he uses rhyme at the conclusion of his sermon to emphasize his theme:

> We have our say now, but come Judgment Day, the questions are going to flow one way. There are going to be some questions on the other side. "Oh, Lord, my life was hard with troubles."
> "Well, did you use it?"
> "Oh Lord, I suffered so."
> "Well, did you choose it?"
> "Lord, I had to hold on so tight to my life" and the question will be "Well, did you lose it?"
> "Lord, my struggles were too hard. I never had a chance."
> And the Lord will ask, "Well, did you dance?"
> When that day comes, there will be no "What about this?" or "that." There will only be "What about you?" There will be no more talk, no more lies, no more complaining. But in that unyielding Power, our finest and weakest hour, we will see the Divine Promise come true.

Rhythm is another tool that is associated mostly with poetry and music. But it is also important to the oral delivery of written material. It has to do with the length of sentences and the emotional quality that language suggests or evokes. As we have seen, the use of polysyndeton and asyndeton has an effect on a sentence's rhythm. Using more conjunctions than expected when listing items can give a sense of their equality or a sense of intensifying rank. Omitting conjunctions can suggest immediacy or energy. Rhythm can also be affected, as noted above, by the selection of assonant and consonant words. Emphasis on vowels allows the speaker to prolong phrases, letting them sing and resonate. Emphasis on consonants can clip one's speech, giving it energy and percussion. In preaching, it is usually good to employ a variety of rhythms. Rhythmical variety will animate a delivery and give emotional shape to a sermon.

When rhythm becomes organized into repeated patterns, it is called *meter*. In certain types of poetry (a sonnet, for instance) and in hymns, the meter needs to be regular and repeated, stanza by stanza. Poets and hymnwriters are concerned with types of meter (iambic, trochaic, dactylic, and so on) and the number of metrical patterns (feet) in each line. Preachers, unless they are using the form of poem or hymn for their sermon, do not need to be concerned with these details of meter. But there is one aspect of meter that can be useful in crafting sermons. Known as *cadence*, it has to do with the way prose sounds when spoken aloud. The cadence of a line can be felt in the way that stressed syllables alternate and combine. Read aloud the following sentence and you will sense its cadence: "WHERE do we LOOK to FIND that FACE, the

COUNTenance uPON the FLESH?" The cadence can be emphasized by lingering on each accented vowel as it is spoken. Selecting words that fall into brief metrical patterns gives spoken language a musical quality. The music of the line is enhanced, say Addonizio and Laux, as "a stressed syllable gets a little push."[71] Writers of prose can learn to work cadence into their work by writing poetry. "So practice on poems," Kilpatrick says. "Most of them will be awful . . . but even the awful ones will help you on the way to better prose."[72] If you take Kilpatrick's advice, you will be in good company. Before he could write a masterpiece like the Gettysburg Address, "Lincoln," says Garry Wills, " . . . began by writing bad poetry."[73]

Exercises in using poetic devices

1. Alliteration, Assonance, and Rhyme: Craft a phrase and, with the help of a thesaurus, substitute alliterative, assonant, and rhyming words that will convey a similar meaning.

   EXAMPLES

   the night fell quickly
   the evening advanced rapidly
   fast fell the night
   daylight sped and night was upon them

   a difficult task
   a demanding duty
   an arduous assignment
   a hard charge
   a laborious chore

2. Rhythm: Describe one event in two different ways. First, suggest tranquillity by using a long sentence filled with vowel-rich words. Second, suggest action and energy by using short phrases and words containing crisp consonants.

   EXAMPLE

   With beaming lights, the automobile turned the corner and wove its way along the swarming boulevard.

   Headlights blazing, the car turned. It sped ahead, zigzagging through the crowded street.

3. Meter and Rhyme: Write a hymn. Begin with a psalm, a free-form poem, or a sermon theme. Paraphrase the original to fit a hymn tune with which you are familiar. Writing your hymn to a known melody will assist you by providing a prescribed meter and rhyme scheme. Be sure that each stanza of the hymn matches the meter of the melody. Also, take care to match accented syllables in the text with the accents in the music. If the melody you choose has a duple meter, the accents will be 1 2, 1 2 or 1 2 3 4. If the tune is in a triple meter, the accents will be 1 2 3, 1 2 3 or 1 2 3 4 5 6.

EXAMPLE

This hymn is an original paraphrase of Psalm 133. It can be sung to the English folk tune O WALY WALY ("The Water Is Wide") or to the hymn tune OLD HUNDREDTH ("Praise God from Whom All Blessings Flow").

How good and pleasing it can be
When people live in unity.
Such peace is precious, fragrant, rare,
Like scented oil upon the hair.

How good and pleasing it can be
When kindred live in harmony;
Refreshing as the sparkling spray
On Zion's mount at break of day.

O brothers, sisters in the Lord
Who seek to live in sweet accord,
The God of peace will surely pour
Such blessings forth forevermore.

COMPLETING THE TASK

The final writing tool that we will examine is *revision.* "Revision is," say Addonizio and Laux,

> the poet's most difficult, demanding, and dangerous work. Difficult because it's hard to let go of our original inspirations or ideas or our best lines, as we may have to do in the service of the poem. Demanding because it calls for us to reach deeper or further than we may want to, or feel we know how to. Dangerous because we feel we might, in the act of trying to make a good poem better, lose touch with the raw energy that drove the poem into its fullness to begin with and destroy what we have so joyously created.[74]

The same is true for the preacher. But we serve not a poem or an inspiration. We serve the gospel and attempt to enable God's people to see Jesus in our work. All the more reason for preachers to revise their material so that it will speak with clarity and depth. There are two lessons that must be learned by beginning preachers. They must learn to focus their work by discovering what needs to be left out. Not every great idea makes its way into a sermon. Some are abandoned. Some are stored for later use. Revision is critical in order to prune a sermon so that it says what needs to be said and nothing more. The second thing that beginning preachers need to learn is that a sermon is not complete when the preacher's ideas have been shaped into a coherent outline. Knowing generally what one wants to say is not the same thing as knowing precisely what you want to say and how you want to say it. One might argue that not all effective preachers write out a manuscript and work its language until it is a carefully crafted artistic artifact. Many great preachers have followed the practice of working on a sermon until they have a general idea of its content and leaving the specifics of expression to the moment of delivery. "Augustine," reports Clyde Fant, ". . . composed by mental preparation, committed his major points to memory, and left the details to the moment."[75] But this is not a model for beginning preachers. Nor is it a model for people who have not learned how to use language well. Certainly, many effective preachers do not work out every jot and tittle and record their work carefully on paper as if their sermons were durable material. But somewhere they have learned to say things with care and have acquired poetic skills so that whether from memory, manuscript, or a moment's inspiration, they will be able to use language that speaks to people of things too deep for words. Revision is the key to putting poetic principles to work. As preachers grow in skill, they may need to spend less time in revision because they spend more time writing poetically in the first place. Like a woodsmith, the wordsmith's tools become more familiar with practice and enable the preacher to craft effective sermons with less uncertainty. For those who wish to preach from memory or preach extemporaneously, the discussion of extemporaneous prayer in the following chapter will provide guidance.

CONCLUSION

In turning to part 2 of this study, we have begun to focus on the aesthetic responsibility of the preacher and the specific ways that preaching is an art. The treasure we have in earthen vessels is the human proclamation of the gospel. Although proclamation may take many forms, its primary form is the spoken word. Whether a sermon makes theological points, brings new insight to a biblical text, or draws people closer to something they already know, it is the use of carefully chosen language and poetic development that enables the discourse of a sermon to function presentationally. It is the poetry of a sermon that enables the preacher to create for worshipers channels of resonance through which deep calls to deep. The preacher, then, is a poet and can learn to draw from the poet's tool bag in order to put into words those things that mere discourse cannot touch.

We have a treasure in the gospel. It is carried forth to God's people in the earthenware of proclamation. The responsibility for bearing that proclamation falls primarily on preachers. The responsibility for publicly bearing our concerns to God is the responsibility of the prayer leader. As we will see in the next chapter, leading public prayer is also an art.

6

The Need as Deep as Life

Eternal Spirit of the living Christ,
I know not how to ask or what to say;
I only know my need, as deep as life,
And only you can teach me how to pray.

Come pray in me the prayer I need this day;
Help me to see your purpose and your will—
Where I have failed, what I have done amiss;
Held in forgiving love, let me be still.

Frank von Christierson

Preaching is one element of worship that calls for carefully crafted language. Because its purpose is to disclose the Divine Presence and proclaim God's promise, it needs to speak with clarity and depth. Another element of worship that requires thoughtful expression is public prayer. People gather in God's presence in the hope and expectation that they will be led into dialogue with their Creator. The substance of that dialogue is not trivial; it has to do with the essentials of human existence. We are concerned, in public prayer, with "needs as deep as life." The purpose of this chapter will be to consider the role of the leader of public prayer, the use of presentational language in prayer, and the issues that relate to leading prayer with hiddenness and performatory power. In particular, our focus will be on those prayers that are not prescribed as *ordinary* parts of a liturgy. We will consider issues relating to those prayers that are prepared as *propers* for a given day or service, such as collects, petitions, intercessions, and pastoral prayers. The presumption is that these prayers are best prepared for each occasion by worship leaders who are part of the worshiping community. Certainly worship books and lectionary aids contain prescribed prayers that can be used by those who lead in

115

prayer. We proceed, however, recognizing that prayers, like sermons, best speak of local needs and concerns when they are prepared by those who are immersed in the life of a worshiping community and can represent the hearts of those who gather.

MESSING WITH PRAYER

The story is told of a country congregation whose custom was to begin each service of worship with a prayer led by a congregational member. The pastor would call out the name of a parishioner, who would then rise, face the congregation, and improvise an invocation. One Sunday morning, the pastor chose to bestow the honor on a reticent man. Cowering in his pew, the man heard his name announced. Slowly, hesitantly, he unfolded his lean limbs, stood, and moved toward the central aisle. He turned to face the congregation, but his gaze was too heavy to lift from the floor. The cap in his hands was kneaded and wrung as the man searched for words with which to lead God's people in prayer. After a silent eternity, the man drew a deep breath, cleared his throat, and spoke softly. "I . . . I reckon I won't mess with it," he said and returned to dissolve into the varnish of his seat.

Leading public prayer is an important responsibility. There is wisdom in knowing whether one has the skills and preparation to undertake the task. But someone has to "mess" with it. The task falls to worship leaders, lay or ordained, who have the training and capacity to lead prayer effectively. In other aspects of communal life, we turn to particular people for leadership. "We naturally look for someone to facilitate, to speak when a chorus of voices would be cacophony, to orchestrate the life of the group, or simply move us through an agenda," says Sister Kathleen Hughes. In the same way, in gathering for prayer we "turn to one among us to orchestrate the movements and order the many gifts."[1] What are the capacities of leadership that make for effective public prayer? Here, as in preaching, we focus on the aesthetic possibilities of prayer leadership. For, just as preaching is an art in that it uses presentational language to give expression to things too deep for words, so corporate prayer relies on nondiscursive language to express things that are as deep as life. This means that those who craft prayers must know something of how language works and its potential for speaking of sentient things. Here again, the writer of public prayers needs to work as a poet.

Does this mean that only beautifully crafted phrases are appropriate for public prayer? C. S. Lewis helps us to see that this is not the case. He suggests that sometimes we need to get away from the beautifully crafted language of authorized worship resources "simply because it is so beautiful and so solemn.

Beauty exalts, but beauty also lulls," he warns.[2] The virtue of working as poet is not to accomplish beautiful expression, but to achieve fresh, clear, penetrating expression. The words of prayer may have beauty. Or they may be disturbing, poignant, or common. But, if they are to be effective words, they will be words that, as Hughes says, "touch the heart and the religious consciousness of those gathered."[3] The purpose of the leader's words will be to speak so clearly of people's gratitude, needs, and concerns that they will "elicit from them their so be it," their "Amen."[4]

Effective leaders of public prayer will approach their task with a sense of aesthetic responsibility for at least two reasons. First, when the many gather in the presence of the One who made them, they turn to the few who lead and offer them hearts and minds that are open to Divine encounter. "Friends, we wish to see Jesus," they say, in a sense. At the time of prayer, what is presented to the worship leader are blank pages of imagination. The people draw quiet and wait for the leader to speak words onto those pages. The leader can place upon them any words that he or she chooses. The assembly trusts that the pages will not be wasted, that the words applied will be pertinent to people's concerns, that the language selected will be that which plumbs the depths of the human needs of those assembled. People trust that they will find resonance with and give consent to the verbal expressions of the leader. They trust also in the work of the Holy Spirit that, through inspiration, discipline, and dedication, the leader of their prayer will be enabled to bring to expression things too deep for their own words. Prayer leaders approach their task as artists not for the sake of demonstrating beautiful language. They do so for the sake of the people who have gathered and for the sake of their faith.

We think of the prayer leader as an artist for another reason. Artists know how to work with symbols, to arrange them in appropriate patterns and prepare well-crafted modes of expression. When they have successfully articulated that which they have conceived, the work of art stands on its own, released from its creator's control, and speaks for the artist as it reaches out to resonate with its percipients. Once the work is prepared and released, the artist becomes invisible and the artistic artifact shows forth.

Leaders of public prayer share the aesthetic responsibility to work in this way. Effective prayer leaders craft their expressions and present them well in order that in performing with excellence, they become invisible. Their words stand forth as that which is primarily perceptible and draw people into the communal conversation with God. Hidden in the shadows of their own work, prayer leaders become transparent to the dialogue they foster. In this process, the aesthetic responsibility of the prayer leader takes on theological purpose: to draw the many who have gathered into conversation with the One who has made them and who can bring divine power to bear on their lives and concerns.

THE LANGUAGE OF PRAYER

Just as with proclamation, the symbols of prayer can take many forms. Certainly music, dance, and gesture can be used as forms of prayer. I once experienced a form of Morning Prayer during which a gifted artist applied black paint strokes to a white canvas while we listened to music. Even though no words were spoken, the participants were drawn into prayerful meditation as we watched the painter carefully execute what he had conceived. The painting seemed abstract in its presentation, a prayer groping for articulation. And then, as the period ended, the painter paused, looked long and thoughtfully at the canvas—like a suspended chord waiting for resolution—and finally applied a single brush stroke. In that instant the anticipated form leapt from the canvas: the crucifixion. We who watched were finally drawn into the fullness of the conversation that the painter was leading with his brush. He said for us something that we did not know to say, but something with which we found resonance.

Most prayer, however, relies on the use of language. Yet, before there are words there is the absence of words: silence. This is the first form of prayer language. Just as a rest in music is not lack of music but part of the complex of musical sound symbols, so silence is part of what we say and part of how we say it in prayer. "Authentic prayer," says Louis Weil, "grows out of a deep interior silence, a still point at which faith looks in love and hope to the One upon whom faith rests."[5] What do you say when the sacred core of your concern aches for expression, but lies beyond the reach of words? At first, you say nothing. The language of corporate prayer is filled with musical rests, with silence. "Let us pray," says the prayer leader, and immediately, there is silence. "Lord, hear our prayer," the people say, and there is another rest. Speech and silence is the rhythm of prayer. They compose the liturgical dialogue in which our deepest exclamations of praise and petition are offered to God and God's first response is returned into the silence.

After the silence there is sound. "Because our human nature communicates meaning through articulated sounds," says Weil, "this silence will overflow into some form, and such forms will usually involve words."[6] When we pray in private, the words may be audible or mere whispers of the imagination. At times, we cannot speak of or even name that which we long to communicate. We open our hearts, bare the flesh of our humanness, and, with the Spirit's assistance, heave heavenward sighs. At other times, as we are able, our prayers take the form of verbal expression, spoken or thought. In public worship, the sound that accompanies the silence is verbal. As we open ourselves in prayer, we trust the leadership of those who speak for us to put into verbal expression the holdings of our hearts. Through the use of careful, well-prepared language, the prayer leader has the capacity and responsibility to speak for us of things that lie at the unfathomable intersection of faith and life.

Those of us who lead public prayer need to remember that our words have power. First, they have, as we have seen, performatory power. They do not merely report something being done but they accomplish it. When we say, "We pray," we are performing the act of drawing the disparate thoughts of a gathered people together and focusing them in the singular act of speaking to God. When we say, in the people's behalf, "Forgive us, Lord," we are laying the sins of a community at the foot of the throne of grace and we are evoking a hope of absolution. We merely say the word and the prayer of the people is accomplished. Second, our words have the power of invoking God's presence and response to our praises and petitions. In worship, the God who made all things attends to our words and brings, as God chooses, that creative power to bear on our concerns. We pray that God will bring understanding, healing, forgiveness, aid, and peace in all manner of human circumstances. Insofar as God responds to public prayer at all, prayer leaders need to see their roles as agents of God's performance in the people's behalf. Finally, our words as leaders of public prayer have the power to speak the unspeakable. Sighs will not do in public prayer. Neither will mere discourse. The matter-of-fact language of ordinary speech is not inauthentic in prayer, but there is a limit to what it can express. We can name certain concerns and list those for whom we pray with prayerful effect. But our responsibility as leaders is to do more. It is to plumb the sentient depths of those gathered, to name anew our humanness, and to draw an assembly of hearts into resonance and conversation with the Creator. To do this, we search for words that will provide presentational expression. We work as poets, selecting according to the logical rightness and necessity of expression those words that best enable us to speak of things too deep for words.

THE SOURCE OF PRAYER LANGUAGE

Where do we find this paradoxical treasure, the words that speak more deeply than words? As leaders of public prayer, we find them first in our own private prayer. To lead others in prayer presumes that the leader has personal experience in speaking with God. Not only is a private prayer life essential to us as disciplined Christians, it is in private devotion that the leader seeks God's assistance in learning to speak for God's people. If preaching is only an attempt to speak God's Word, then public prayer is only an attempt to speak the people's word to God. We pray, as leaders, that God will be present in our speech and attentive to our words. We pray also that the Holy Spirit be present in the dialogue we lead in order that through our carefully crafted expressions we can sing with solidarity the song of those we represent.

Second, we find words for prayer through our powers of perception. In the last chapter, we saw that perception is the first tool of the poet. That power is as important to leaders of prayer as it is for preachers, for they, too, have the responsibility of knowing the circumstances of local context. If there is joy in the community, God's people will want to be led in prayers of thanksgiving. If there is sorrow or tragedy in the congregation, the community, the nation, or the world, the people will expect that someone will help them to speak of these things to God. Beyond knowing the outlines of local and pertinent situations, the perceptive prayer leader will be attuned to the workings of the senses. How does sorrow feel? How is one kind of joy different from another kind of joy? What do cold, coolness, warmth, and heat feel like? In order to give accurate expression to the real circumstances of worshiping people, the perceptive prayer leader needs to look carefully at the world and then seek language that brings felt things to life. Like the preacher, though perhaps more briefly, the person who leads in public prayer has the capacity to create virtual life for those who join in prayer. This can only be done by people who know what real life looks like.

Our presumption, again, is that the leader of public prayer is preparing to lead fresh prayers. Prayers that are found in worship books, lectionary aids, and bulletin inserts[7] can serve as helpful models of prayer and provide examples of prayer forms. But petitions that are written by people removed from the worshiping community and prepared for publication will not have the immediate power of prayers that are crafted by worship leaders who live and worship within a faith community. Kathleen Hughes reminds us that "there is no such thing as a 'generic' celebration. Each time we begin to shape prayer, the needs and expectations of a very concrete community must be taken into account."[8] The prayer leader will, says Dietrich Bonhoeffer agreeably, "have to share the daily life of the fellowship; he [or she] must know the cares, the needs, the joys and thanksgivings, the petitions and the hopes of others. Their work and everything they bring with them must not be unknown."[9] Only those who live and worship among the assembled can perceive closely and accurately the lives of those whose prayer they lead.

The third place we look to find language for prayer is in the heart. Whether public prayer is prepared in advance of a service or composed in the moment, whether it is in the form of lengthy and eloquent address or brief call and response, it will be language of the heart. As leaders of public prayer, we pray for God's guidance, we look carefully at the world around us, but in the end, we simply speak what is on our hearts. We may not personally experience the joys and concerns of all those whom we lead in prayer, but we take their feelings to heart and address them with our words in ways that resonate with their circumstances. We use language that is simple, ordinary, and authentic. But we attempt to use that language in extraordinary ways to give expression to those impenetrable things that are as deep as life.

FRESH LANGUAGE FOR PRAYER

Many prayers have stood the test of time and continue to speak for us from what Kathleen Hughes calls "the place of our humanity."[10] Prayers such as the Lord's Prayer; "Make me an instrument of thy peace," attributed to Saint Francis; and "God be in my head," from the *Sarum Primer*, communicate with timeless ingenuity. Most of the prayers we compose will not have such durability. Nor will they, in weeks and years, seem as up-to-date as when they were first crafted. Language changes; human circumstances change. Our prayers also need to change, to keep abreast of life.

Like poetry and preaching, public prayer has the capacity to give fresh expression to elements of human circumstance. It also has the potential to give an assembly of prayerful people new ways to envision the God to whom they pray. Stock phrases, hackneyed expressions, overused images do not retain the power to help us see deeply, to articulate that which is vitally felt, or to know the fullness of the God who is our partner in conversation. Consider, for example, this formula that is ponderously used in certain pietistic traditions: "Lord, we *just* ask," or "Lord, we *just* pray." Rather than drawing participants more fully into the rich possibilities of God's interaction with people, the heavy repetition of the word "just" dulls the imagination and diminishes the listener's expectation of divine response by suggesting that the prayer request is insignificant. In such cases, simply removing the surplus "justs" will strengthen the prayers in two ways. First, it acknowledges the full boldness of our prayers as we call on God's presence and power. Commenting on the overuse of this word in prayer, William Willimon once quipped, "No, we are not asking God for much. *Just* resurrection from the dead!" Second, removing the qualifying "just" emphasizes the daring expectation of divine response. When we pray, we are not merely whining to God about our concerns. We pray with full expectation that God is faithful and will deliver on the promise of peace, comfort, forgiveness, and salvation.

Other commonplace prayer images can also work contrary to the purpose of public worship. While the image of God as Father is normative in many traditions, its overuse abrades in some settings and can distract people from prayer. On the other hand, whereas the image of God as Mother is helpful innovation in some settings, it is jarring elsewhere. The challenge for us as people who lead in public prayer is to find fresh language for our work so that those who pray with us are freed to give assent to our naming of their circumstances and enabled to envision new dimensions of divine possibility.

In searching for new language for prayer we can turn to the poetic tools that we examined in the preceding chapter. Using them will involve experimentation. The only way, says Brian Wren, "to find out about metaphors and similes is to make them and see where they lead, and how well they can be expressed in liturgical speech. . . ."[11] Wren experiments with workshop participants by asking them to brainstorm about images of God. He wove the results of one brainstorming session into the text of new hymn called "Are You the Friendly God?"

> Are you the friendly God, shimmering, swirling, formless,
> nameless and ominous, Spirit of brooding might,
> presence beyond our sense, all-embracing night,
> the hovering wings of warm and loving darkness?
> If hope will listen, love will show and tell,
> and all shall be well, all manner of things be well.[12]

Borrowing from the approach of Brian Wren and from the poetic tools of our previous chapter, leaders of public prayer can learn to experiment with language and create new expressions for our public conversations with God and new images for our address to the One in whose presence we gather. The following exercises may provide a starting point for such experimentation.

Exercises

1. Images for God: To expand one's lexicon of Divine address, consider verbs that indicate Divine activity as typically invoked in prayer. Pair these verbs with corresponding metaphoric images for God that can serve as elements of address. A useful technique is to look up the verb in a thesaurus, seeking synonyms to use as resources for crafting corresponding images.

    EXAMPLES

    healing: Restorer, Touching God, Mending Presence
    enlightening: Illuminator, Teacher, Guiding Spirit
    forgiving: Compassionate One, Spirit of Release, Liberating Word
    providing: Fount of Favor, Abundant God, Provident One
    caring: Great Awareness, God of Vigilance, Attendant One
    sustaining: Bearer of Life, Nourishing Spirit
    comforting: Soothing Word, Spirit of Solace, Consoling Presence

2. Images for God: Extract biblical images from the Scripture lessons appointed for the service of worship. Use them to create corresponding

forms of address that coordinate the liturgical dialogue of prayer with the proclamation of God's Word.

EXAMPLES

Luke 9:28–36 (The Transfiguration)
  O God of the Mountain, O Lord of the Height
Acts 2:1–13 (The Coming of the Holy Spirit)
  Blazing Spirit, Flame of God, Holy Tempest, Divine Turbulence
Psalm 46 ("Be still and know that I am God.")
  Spirit of Quietness, Silent Word, Resting Presence, God
  of Disturbance and Tranquillity
Romans 8:14–17 ("For all who are led by the Spirit of God are children of God.")
  Parenting Spirit, Adopting God, God Who Claims Us

3. Metonyms and Synecdoches for human situations: Considering the human conditions for which we typically pray, identify related circumstances, elements, or symptoms that can stand for the original condition. Craft phrases that might be used in prayer.

EXAMPLES

hunger: hollow stomachs
  "Abundant God, we pray that hollowness shall cease . . ."
fear: trembling
  "Send, O Resting Presence, your tremble-easing peace . . ."
sense of loss: an ache
  "The vacant ache is looming, God, where yesterday was joy . . ."
death: loss of body temperature; loss of breath
  "When coldness comes and breath is spent . . ."

EXTEMPORANEOUS PRAYER

The careful crafting of the language of public prayer suggests that prayer leaders compose their prayers in advance of their being spoken. Preparing in this way provides for maximum control regarding language and content. But, as with preaching, some speakers are able to communicate effectively using extemporized speech. The benefit of drawing one's preparation into the moment of delivery is that it allows for the prayers to address the most immediate of circumstances. One lay prayer leader of my acquaintance is known for crafting prayers that draw thematic elements from the sermon as if she had read the sermon in advance. She accomplishes this by taking notes on the sermon as it is preached and folding its motifs into the prayers that soon follow. The result is that people are drawn into a dialogue that flows naturally from God's Word as it has been preached to a response that has been properly ordered to the specific themes of proclamation. Not all prayer leaders will have the capacity to absorb and synthesize ideas so quickly as to facilitate such immediate conversation. Yet, due to the fluid nature of public worship, the unanticipated need for extemporized prayer may arise. During times set aside for the free prayers of the assembly, a person may be drawn to speak of an unexpected concern or a newly discovered need. Or the minister might choose to conclude the prayers with improvised intercessions that address developing circumstances. And ministers, lay and ordained, can expect to be called on to lead in public prayer in paraliturgical assemblies such as Bible studies and communal meals. For leaders who wish to extemporize effective prayers, preparation and forethought are crucial.

A model for extemporized prayer leadership can be found in the work of improvisational musicians. A hallmark of the jazz idiom is the improvised solo. Within the parameters of a song's rhythm, meter, and chordal progression, individual singers and instrumentalists take their turn at creating spontaneous musical articulation. Often demonstrating great creativity and skill, these cascades of innovation are accomplished by musicians who have carefully studied and practiced the canons of improvisational theory. The elaborate intervals, steps, and leaps, the repeated and transposed sequences, the complementary and contrasting melodic motifs, the aptly borrowed musical phrases, and the felicitously woven inventions of sound derive not from the genius of a moment's inspiration. They are elements of improvisational technique that are learned and practiced until they are available to the musician as ready building blocks of extemporization. Just as speakers acquire a linguistic vocabulary, jazz musicians acquire a vocabulary of musical idioms. They learn to play facilely in every diatonic key, both major and minor, and in each of the ancient church modes (such as Dorian and Phrygian). They also learn standardized phrases and practice playing them in every key. In addition, they learn the rudiments of jazz harmonization and substitution, chord progression, and instrumental voicing. Once they have acquired a musical vocabulary and understand its improvisational grammar, they practice its use until, without hesitation, they can step up to an eight- or sixteen-bar solo break and fill it with melismatic invention. Another form of improvisational music is organ invention. Like their jazz counterparts, organists also learn the canons of improvisation until they can spontaneously create a prelude on a hymn tune or provide spiraling variations on a melodic theme. What prayer leaders can learn from these musical analogs is that successful improvisation does not occur without painstaking preparation and practice.

All too frequently, extemporized public prayer is halting and clumsy, such as this: "Gracious God, . . . we, ah, we humbly pray that you, um . . . bring healing to those who have, ah, . . . to those whose spirits are broken or . . . distressed." Such prayer defeats the leader's purpose. Rather than artfully drawing into the shadows allowing the words to speak plainly the prayer of the people, the leader interposes his or her ineptitude and helps people to see, not Jesus, but plainly and embarrassingly, him or herself. Those who have the ability to offer extemporaneous prayer effectively are those who have learned the vocabulary of prayer and practiced its use.

To acquire such a prayer vocabulary and facility in its use, prayer leaders can turn to a variety of sources. First, of course, is Scripture. One can practice crafting prayer by speaking aloud the psalms and the prayers of the Old and New Testaments. Speaking them aloud will rehearse and ingrain proven patterns of language and form so that as they become familiar, they are positioned for ready use by the imagination. Another source for a prayer vocabulary is, as previously suggested, the published prayers of worship books and devotional material. Again, using these prayers as models and speaking them aloud is helpful practice for spontaneous verbalization. Another fruitful source for learning the language of prayer is the body of Christian hymnody. Old hymn texts that have grown favored because of their peculiar ability to express the praise and petition of God's people or new hymn texts that provide fresh imagery and new insight as to issues of faith and life are rich resources. Even as most of the musical idioms that are memorized and employed for jazz improvisation are standardized and borrowed, so fresh language for improvised prayer can derive from the inventions of others who have mastered the ability to use creative language for the sake of the faith of God's people. Finally, further practice in expanding the vocabulary of prayer comes as prayer leaders give careful attention to crafting original turns of phrase that bring fresh expression to the sentient elements of faith and life. Speaking these innovations aloud in one's private prayer life provides the kind of experimentation and testing that is advocated by Brian Wren and the practice that improvisation requires.

Exercise

1. Turning to the psalms and collections of hymns, make a list of creative images that name God, refer to elements of human circumstance, or suggest modes of praise. Practice using these prayer idioms by speaking them aloud. Using the list as a visual cue, practice improvising prayers of praise and intercession in various forms.

   EXAMPLES OF IMAGES FOR GOD FROM THE PSALMS

   The One Who sits in the Heavens (Ps. 2:4)
   God of Darkness, God of Brightness, God of Thunder, God of Breath (Ps. 18)
   Distant God (Ps. 22:1)
   Great Voice of Thunder, Voice of Peace (Ps. 29)
   Timeless God (Ps. 90:2, 4)

Creator of Song and Object of Praise (Ps. 96)
O God, the Joy of Faithful Hearts (Ps. 128)
Searching and Knowing God (Ps. 139)

EXAMPLES OF IMAGES FOR GOD FROM HYMNS

Maker and Monarch (from "Brightest and Best of the Stars of the Morning," by Reginald Heber)
Jesus, Refuge of the Weary (from "Jesus, Refuge of the Weary," by Girolamo Savonarola, tr. Jane F. White)
Lord of Years (from "Crown Him with Many Crowns," by Matthew Bridges)
Victim Divine (from "Victim Divine, Your Grace We Claim," by Charles Wesley)
O Fount of Grace (from "O Bread of Life from Heaven," Latin Hymn)
Divine Instructor (from "Father of Mercies, in Your Word," by Anne Steele)
Sun of Righteousness; Dayspring from on High; Daystar (from "Christ, Whose Glory Fills the Sky," by Charles Wesley)
Light-Creator, Light of Light Begotten, and Light-Revealer (from "Thy Strong Word," by Martin Franzmann)

EXAMPLES OF IMAGES FOR HUMAN CONDITIONS FROM THE PSALMS

Lions lurk to sieze the poor (Ps. 10:9)
An army encamped against us (Ps. 26:3)
Eyes wasting away from grief (Ps. 31:9)
Wounds that grow foul and fester; to be utterly spent and crushed; suffering tumult of the heart; friends and neighbors standing far off (Ps. 38)
Anointed with the oil of gladness (Ps. 45:7)
Speech smoother than butter, but a heart set on war; words softer than oil, but are, in fact, drawn swords (Ps. 55:21)
Fortunes restored like rivers in a dry land (Ps. 126:4)
A calmed and quieted soul is like a weaned child with its mother (Ps. 131:2)

EXAMPLES OF IMAGES FOR HUMAN CONDITIONS FROM HYMNS

When, repentant to the skies, scarce we lift our weeping eyes (from "Savior, When in Dust to You," by Robert Grant)
When the woes of life o'er-take us, hopes deceive, and fears annoy (from "In the Cross of Christ I Glory," by John Bowring)
With forbidden pleasures should this vain world charm (from "In the Hour of Trial," by James Montgomery)
When our hearts are wintry, grieving or in pain (from "Now the Green Blade Rises," by John M. C. Crum)
Dressed no more in spirit somber, clothed instead with joy and wonder (from "Now We Join in Celebration," by Joel W. Lundeen)
May we arise pure and fresh and sinless (from "Now the Day Is Over," by Sabine Baring-Gould)

Bind hearts in true devotion, endless as the seashore's sands, boundless
as the deepest ocean (from "Hear Us Now, Our God and Father," by
Harry N. Huxhold)
Take away the love of sinning (from "Love Divine, All Loves Excelling,"
by Charles Wesley)

EXAMPLES OF IDIOMS OF PRAISE FROM THE PSALMS

My heart is glad, my soul rejoices (Ps. 16:9)
It is you who light my lamp, O God (Ps. 18:28)
I will sing and make melody to the LORD (Ps. 27:6)
My heart overflows with a goodly theme (Ps. 45:1)
The hills gird themselves with joy; the valleys deck themselves with
grain, they shout and sing together for joy (Ps. 65:12–13)
Let the sea roar, and all that fills it; let the floods clap their hands for joy
(Ps. 98:7–8)
Awake my soul; awake, O harp and lyre, awake the dawn (Ps. 108:1–2)
The unsearchable greatness of God (Ps. 145:3)

EXAMPLES OF IDIOMS OF PRAISE FROM HYMNS

With high delight let us unite in songs of sweet jubilation (from "With
High Delight Let Us Unite," by Georg Vetter, tr. Martin Franzmann)
We sing when love-possessed (from "When Morning Gilds the Skies,"
German hymn, tr. Robert Bridges)
Our Lord, we do not merit the favor you have shown, and all our souls
and spirits bow down before your throne (from "O Living Bread from
Heaven," by Johann Rist, tr. Catherine Winkworth)
Let every kindred, every tribe on this celestial ball praise you, Lord of
all (from "All Hail the Power of Jesus' Name," by Edward Perronet)
Let streets and homes with praises ring (from "Christ Is Alive! Let
Christians Sing," by Brian Wren)
Tune our hearts to sing your praise (from "Come, Thou Fount of Every
Blessing," by Robert Robinson)
To you, great One in Three, eternal praises be (from "Come, Thou
Almighty King," source unknown)
Fill the heavens with sweet accord (from "Holy God, We Praise Your
Name," source unknown, tr. Clarence A. Walworth)

THE SHAPE OF THE DIALOGUE

In order for leaders of public prayer to perform their task well, to draw people into conversation with their creator, and to speak with clarity and invoca-
tional power, they should keep in mind several principles that have to do with
the shape of the prayer dialogue. The first has to do with the direction of the
conversation.

1) Public prayer is addressed to God. In the reading of Scripture and in
preaching, the speaker is using his or her voice as a vehicle for bringing God's

Word to the people. The direction of address is from God to the assembly. In public prayer, the direction is reversed. The leader's voice now speaks a word from the people to God. A commonly heard mistake is for the prayer leader to use the time of prayer to speak, not to God, but, in disguised fashion, to the people. This typically happens in two ways. One form of this problem occurs when prayer leaders use the moment of prayer to make announcements to the assembly: "We pray, O God, for Wilbur Anderson, who undergoes heart bypass surgery this coming Wednesday, and for Mary Brannigan, who is recovering at St. Mary's Hospital from a car accident." Filling prayers with announcements is inappropriate for two reasons. First, it wrongly suggests that God is unaware of the concerns of those for whom we pray and needs a reminder. Second, the practice misuses the assembly's attitude of prayer and misdirects their attention. Leaders cannot expect worshipers to be drawn into a dynamic dialogue with their Creator in which they attend to needs as deep as life, while simultaneously attending to the reception of detailed information. A better approach is to use the time of public prayer for addressing the people's concerns to God and finding other times to speak directly to the people about items of community concern. Suggestions about how to deal with prayer announcements will be offered in the next chapter.

The second form of this mistake occurs when the prayer leader uses the time of prayer to hurl exhortations over his or her shoulder at the unprepared assembly. For example: "Receive, O God, the service of your people who need to rise from the couch of their indifference and employ their hands in charitable acts in behalf of the hungry, the homeless, and the oppressed." Clearly, in this example, the point of the address is not to invoke God's assistance, but to motivate the assembly to greater service. Such statements are moralist harangues thinly disguised as prayer. They are, as William Willimon calls them, "sermonettes with eyes closed."[13] For prayer leaders to speak in this way is inappropriate because it abuses the trust given them by those who have bowed heads and hearts to speak and be open to God.

2) *Public prayer is corporate prayer.* Public prayer is not the private prayer of a leader offered in public. "Your job as [leader]," says Willimon, "is not to give the people your prayer, but to lead them in their prayer."[14] I once was asked by parishioners to speak a word of pastoral reproval to a prayer leader whose prayers were crafted with beauty and imagination. The problem was her prayers made people uncomfortable because they seemed to be the kind of prayers that one would pray in the privacy of a bedroom. A reminder to her about the corporate nature of worship helped her to recast her petitions in language that was less intimate and more inclusive. To craft prayers that engage

all people, the leader should avoid the use of personal pronouns (I, me, mine) and avoid making people the subject of predicate phrases (serve the Lord, be faithful, remember the imprisoned, etc.). Instead, using plural pronouns, the leader should speak in the imperative using verbs that focus on what God can do, for example: "We ask, O God, that you *teach* us to serve you, *guide* us in faithfulness, and *help* us to remember those in need."

3) *Public prayer is inclusive.* Common violations of this principle are the use of gender-specific pronouns in reference to all people and the use of language that dishonors categories of people. Because much has been written to encourage liturgical language that is inclusive, irrespective of gender, age, physical ability, and race, we will confine our consideration to a less addressed concern. Worshipers are potentially excluded from corporate prayer when leaders incorporate personal opinion into their petitions. Even if an opinion is thought to be universally held or biblically based, it has no place in public prayer. A prayer leader cannot assume that all worshipers hold the same convictions that he or she holds or that others interpret Scripture as they do. Nor is it the responsibility of the prayer leader to enlighten the assembly as to "the Christian stance" on current social and political concerns. The prayer leader's task is to speak so as to bring people's concerns to God through the use of petitions crafted to elicit the people's "Amen." "I was uncomfortable again in chapel today," quipped worship professor Michael Aune. "During the Prayers of the People we had to vote on the petitions." Given the wide-ranging commonalities of human circumstance, prayer leaders can search for modes of expression that allow all people to resonate with their words. Exclusion might be self-imposed, as occurs when a worshiper is reluctant to engage in the dialogue or unwilling to be repentant during a prayer for forgiveness. But exclusion must not be imposed by the one who has the responsibility to draw the disparate voices of the assembly together in the univocal act of prayer. This does not mean that a prayer leader's sensitivity for political or social issues be set aside when crafting prayers. Certainly political and social issues are fitting subjects for prayerful consideration and Divine address. But prayers dealing with these issues need to be crafted in ways that lead God's people to consider the possibilities of Divine response in the face of institutional problems. Thus, it would be inappropriate to offer either "God, forgive our nation for invading Iraq" or "God, keep us from destroying all the old-growth redwoods." Instead, when ordered to reflect biblical themes, the issues can be most appropriately addressed: "O God of Peace, guide our nation in its world affairs and help us to find ways to live in harmony, even with those who seem to be our enemies" and "Great Creator, teach us to care for all your creation and to use our dominion over the woodlands wisely."

CONCLUSION

Like many aspects of worship, leading public prayer is an art. It uses presentational symbols to express people's praise and concerns that are as deep as life. Without the use of presentational symbols, we face the possibility that prayer will fail in helping people address those things too deep for words. Messing with public prayer is no simple matter. The effective prayer leader attends to careful use of language and draws on poetic tools for the creation of forms that engage the assembly and unite people's hearts in prayer. Whether choosing to craft prayers in advance or to pray extemporaneously, performing this ministry with fresh, pertinent, probing language will prepare one to deal well with this critical element of worship.

The final aspect of liturgical expression that we will consider is the use of language by those who speak words to guide the assembly throughout the course of worship. These are not God's Word addressed to God's people, nor the people's word addressed to God. These miscellaneous words of worship leadership are the words of the few directed to the many for the sake of effecting graceful and engaging worship. As we shall see in the final chapter, there is also a need for these liturgical directions to be rendered with aesthetic care.

In the Shadow of the Cross

Beneath the cross of Jesus, I long to take my stand;
The shadow of a mighty rock within a weary land,
A home within a wilderness, a rest upon the way,
From the burning of the noontide heat and burden of the day.
. . . .
I take, O cross, your shadow for my abiding place;
I ask no other sunshine than the sunshine of his face;
Content to let the world go by, to know no gain or loss,
My sinful self my only shame, my glory all, the cross.

Elizabeth C. Clephane

The chief symbol of the Christian faith is the cross. Not so for Reformed Christians of Hungary. For historical reasons their churches avoid using the symbol that speaks so strongly to the rest of the Christian world. During the Counter-Reformation in Hungary, as Roman church authorities sought to force Reformed Christians to recant their theological stance, the cross was used as a tool of persuasion and a sign of compliance. Those who, by means of torture, recanted were made to kiss the cross to signify their return to the Roman fold. For this reason, even today, Reformed Hungarian Christians view the cross not as a symbol of liberation from sin or the power of Christ. For them it remains a sign that their church was persecuted. In place of the cross, they install a star on their steeples, vestments, and paraments. As a central symbol, the star speaks on many levels, of faith and faithfulness, of persecution and suffering, of triumph over death, and of the hope they place in the One who is the bright morning star of John's revelation.

The use of symbols is the way we speak of human circumstance. Some things can be spoken of by virtue of discursive symbols. Other things are too

deep, too painful, or too intense to use words. Presentational symbols are the
tools we use when, as Aidan Kavanagh says, "reality swamps all other forms of
discourse."[1] When does this occur? It happens regularly, Kavanagh says,
"when one approaches God with others, as in the liturgy."[2]

Liturgy is filled with nondiscursive symbols that speak for us. Whether we
use crosses, stars, vestments, furniture, images, movements, music, or speech,
the presentational symbols of the liturgy speak in ways that mere discourse
cannot. In fact, the rituals of liturgy are not only composed of symbols, but
they are symbols themselves which speak of those things that are soul-deep.
As we saw in chapter 1, the rituals of worship exhibit a sense of "virtual experience." They do what all art does. They draw us into their virtual world and
create the semblance of felt things. Rituals symbolize, says Louis Dupre,

> joyful and sad occasions but never turn joyful or sad themselves. They
> express love without passion, austerity without hardship, sorrow with-
> out grief. Rites articulate real life, they mold it into their restrictive
> forms but they never fully merge with it.[3]

The rituals of liturgy are, as Don Saliers has called them, "art for the long
haul," that is, they provide the church with prayerful and engaging symbolic
actions that enable God's people to gather in the name and the promise of
"God's self-giving incarnate act."[4]

The power of presentational symbols, as we have seen, is in their ability to
address aspects of human reality that are too deep for ordinary language. They
speak for themselves. A painter creates a painting that speaks for the artist in
ways that he or she cannot otherwise articulate. A composer cannot verbally
describe the power and movement of his or her composition. It must be heard
for itself. "If a poet must explain the poem before it is recited," observes Aidan
Kavanagh, "there is something wrong with the poem."[5] The same can be said
of the rituals of worship. Kavanagh warns that "if a liturgy must be explained
before it is done, there must be something wrong with the liturgy."[6] The rituals of worship speak for themselves. If done well, they do not need explanation or to be filled with miscellaneous commentary in order to make them flow
smoothly or accomplish their purpose. The symbol of the cross speaks more
clearly and on more levels than any discursive explanation could indicate.
Those who live in the shadow of the cross know that words could not replace
its power as an expression of their faith. Those who embrace the virtual experience of worship know that no amount of liturgical chatter can deepen their
worship experience or explain the power of its images, gestures, movements,
music, and speech.

This is important for worship leaders to understand. Their role is to facilitate the ritual, not to keep up a running commentary. They need to approach

their task with aesthetic sensitivity so that, through careful planning and execution, they remain hidden in order for the rituals of worship to speak for themselves. Worship leaders need to work as artists, creating forms that articulate things too deep for words, forms that draw people into solidarity with others as they come into God's presence and experience God's power and promise. Certainly, they take center stage on occasion. Certainly, they speak, as the ritual demands. Certainly they move and embody the ritual. But all is done that they might serve as Philip to those who gather, leading them into an encounter with the Hidden One even as they move gracefully into the shadows. Living and working in the shadow of the cross: that is the abiding place of those who lead public worship. The purpose of this chapter is to consider artful ways to deal with the general elements of worship that call for expressive leadership.

THE LANGUAGE OF RITUAL

We have discussed at length the need for preachers and prayer leaders to craft their language with aesthetic and poetic care. But the language of ritual employs more than verbal expression. It also involves the use of the body in terms of movement and gesture, the arrangement of the liturgical environment, the use of music, and many other symbols. In the rituals of worship, we encounter God and respond to God in ways that wholly involve us. Evelyn Underhill says it this way:

> Incited by God, dimly or sharply conscious of the obscure pressure of God, we respond to God best not by a simple movement of the mind, but by a rich and complex action, in which our whole nature is concerned, and which has at its full development the characters of a work of art. We are framed for an existence which includes not only thought and speech, but gesture and manual action; and when we turn Godward, our life here will not be fully representative of our nature, nor will our act of worship be complete, unless all these forms of expression find a place in it. Our religious action must . . . link every sense with that element of our being which transcends and coordinates sense, so that the whole of our nature plays its part in our total response to the Unseen.[7]

The forms of expression that find a place in ritual are many. Each needs to be executed responsibly. Let us look briefly at several forms of ritual language with a view toward understanding how they can be performed artfully. As in the use of speech, the purpose of careful execution is not that God demands our best. Nor is it for the sake of the performance nor for artistic reasons. These things are done well for theological purpose. We seek excellence for the sake of the faith of God's people, in order to reach them, to touch them deeply, and to articulate things of the heart.

Gesture is a ritual language. Here again is the paradox: We gesture in ritual so as to be seen. But, at the same time, we are to remain transparent. The goal is, as Kavanagh describes it, to be "like a Zen master" who is as "'uninteresting' as a glass of cold, clear, nourishing water."[8]

Gestures in worship are to be seen for the purpose of allowing the leader to be hospitable,[9] expressive, and effective. Hospitality suggests that the worship leader is equally available to all people in the assembly. Just as the preacher adjusts his or her volume so as to be heard by those in every seat, the leader's gestures must be appropriate to the size of the worship space and visible to all. Hospitality also suggests that gestures be open and expansive, in order to welcome and invite people to participate in worship. Expressiveness suggests that gestures are clear signals of the leader's intentions. Like the preacher who searches for the right word, the worship leader should practice gestures and search for appropriate modes of physical expression. If gestures are clear and visible, they will be effective modes of communication that draw people into participation in worship's unfolding actions. Because they speak for themselves, effective gestures help to keep worship from being cluttered by extraneous prattle.

For ritual gestures to be hospitable, expressive, and effective, they should be made naturally and with grace. Although many kinds of gestures might be considered, a single form of gesture, with slight variations, can serve most of a worship leader's communicative needs. Extending the arms outward, to the side, with palms facing upward is a gesture that is naturally made, easily varied as to its size, and useful in a variety of ways. Used as an accompaniment to a spoken greeting, it is a sign of welcome. Used along with a verbal invitation to prayer, it is a sign of inclusion. The same gesture can be used in the place of a verbal command as an invitation for the people to stand. If they are standing, it can also be used to invite them to be seated. Using this simple gesture helps the worship leader avoid voicing awkward phrases such as "Will you please rise for the singing of the Gospel acclamation?" or inhospitable commands such as "Be seated." The gesture also allows the worship leader to avoid using the ungraceful palm-down squashing motion as a way to get people seated.

Movement is a ritual language. Gesture is one type of ritual movement. There are several others that allow ministers to add expression to their ritual leadership. Dance and signing are two forms of ritual movement that communicate on many levels. Discussion of their techniques is beyond the scope of this chapter and well beyond the capacity of this writer. We can, however, fruitfully consider two other types of ritual movement. The first is simply moving from one place to another in order to engage in different activities during the course of worship. Movement should be made smoothly, with forethought and intention. Worshipers are distracted by leaders who move about without apparent reason or who stumble about the chancel. Jana Childers says that movement in the sanctuary "trumps" all other ritual activities:

> A bright red parament, a person speaking in a loud voice, somebody reading the Word of God aloud, a soloist singing, or even a whole choir going all out, can easily be upstaged by somebody walking. The congregation's attention will always be drawn to movement and will always and forever be drawn to movement that suggests that there is something unexpected going on.[10]

Ritual movement always communicates something. What it communicates may be positive, such as a leader's sense of purpose or confidence in his or her role. It may also communicate something negative: confusion or lack of familiarity with the space. Practice and restraint can guide leaders to move carefully and sparingly as they seek to be transparent in their roles.

Another form of ritual movement is procession. The power of procession is meaningfully demonstrated in this poem by Janet Schlichting:

> What is procession?
> Movement from place to place,
> measured movement, stately movement,
> a representative few treading a representative distance:
> journey distilled.
> This is what all journeys are, it proclaims,
> this is journey at its heart.
>
> Again and again,
> from week to week,
> from age to age,
> there is something of endings and beginnings;
> of closing doors behind and opening those ahead,
> of meeting and walking together.
>
> What is procession? A journey, distilled.
>
> From age to age, from east to west
> we have skipped and limped and marched and run
> and shuffled and strolled our various ways.
> Our stories reverberate in measured tread.
>
> From age to age, from east to west
> our hurried feet have marked
> the peaks and valleys, the sand and stone,
> the mud, the grass, the dust,
> the streams.
> We pause in solemn pace to remember:

all ground is holy ground.
We come interiorly shoeless.

What is procession?

It is journey distilled—journey at its heart,
a gathering into one movement
of a church on the way:
a pilgrim people, a dusty, longing people,
yet walking with head high;
knowing ourselves, showing ourselves
to be the royal nation, the holy people
won by the Son,
called by his word,
gathered around his table.
There we discover again,
from age to age, from east to west,
for all our journeys,
the source, the ground, the companion, the way.[11]

Those representative few who are involved in this distilled journey have a responsibility to the many: to move with dignity, reverence, and grace. Their role is to engage in what J. D. Crichton calls the "solemn dance"[12] as a ritual means of naming the journey that stands for all our journeys. Like all dances, it is choreographed and rehearsed in order that it might draw people into its ritual memory. Also, processions, "whether penitential or festive," as Kavanagh reminds us, "need . . . elements of ritual and artistic flair, as one so often sees in secular parades, trooping of colors, and even funeral corteges."[13]

Repetition and rhythm are elements of ritual language. Folksinger Chuck Collins once remarked that the verses of a song exist only as an excuse for people to keep singing a wonderful refrain. He knew that there is value and meaning in going over familiar territory. In worship, we repeat certain movements, regularly sing songs that form a liturgical setting, recite prayers and creeds from memory, and respond with repeated phrases in litanies and psalms. The repetitions of ritual and the rhythms of their recurrence do more than entertain us. They shape us as we rehearse their themes, engage us as we enter into their familiarity, and draw us to deeper levels of understanding as we speak, sing, or enact them by rote. There is a difference between using hackneyed phrases in prayer and preaching and the repetition of ritual phrases in worship. Whereas stale language in preaching and in prayer fails to engage and fire the imagination, the repetition of carefully chosen liturgical phrases gives the imagination a home. From there it can soar to heights or delve to depths, seeking and creating new layers of meaning.

Music is a ritual language. The vast topic of music as a mode of ritual communication can hardly be addressed in a single book. But, for the purpose of offering guidance to ministers who wish to use their voices in musical leadership, the following observations may be useful:

1) If you can speak effectively, you can learn to sing effectively. Those who have been told that they have a "tin ear" or that they "cannot carry a tune in a bucket" are generally people who do *not* have an aural or vocal deficiency. Typically, they are people who have not learned to use the ear to guide their vocal production. In repeated experiments with non-singers, I have learned that even the people who are most skeptical about their musical abilities are able to demonstrate that their ears can distinguish relationships between pitches. If a person has the capacity to hear pitch relationships, he or she can learn to match pitches and sing melodies by using the ear to provide feedback for the voice. Worship leaders who wish to learn to chant or lead others in song can do so, as long as they have a voice that can speak, an ear that can listen to others and to themselves, and the desire to practice using voice and ears as partners in creating musical sound. It takes a lot of work for the so-called "tone-deaf" to acquire useful leadership skills. But it can be done by those whose desire to do so outweighs their fear of singing in public. A key to overcoming this problem is finding a patient, encouraging vocal coach who believes in the possibility that all voices can be tuned for praise.

2) The best singers do not necessarily make the best cantors and song leaders. The anecdote in chapter 2 regarding the chanting of the operatic singer demonstrates the problem for good singers. Singing with virtuosity draws undue attention to the vocal gifts of the worship leader. For gifted singers, the words of John Bell in his instructions to song leaders may be helpful: "sing a bit worse than your best and always use your normal voice."[14] Those who have average vocal ability often make fine cantors because they naturally do things that better singers have grown beyond. They sing with a natural voice, in a comfortable range, and avoid the excessive use of resonance. And they often sing without vibrato, the gentle, rhythmic undulation of pitch that is natural to experienced singers. Vibrato is an unnecessary vocal adornment for chanting psalms and leading responsorial service music. (But remember, singing without vibrato makes it crucial for the singer to stay precisely on pitch.)

3) Breath control is crucial. Breath is the fuel of the voice. Learning to breathe correctly is fundamental to any successful public use of the voice. Speakers, singers, and cantors all benefit from efficiently drawing their lungs full of air and carefully regulating its use. "Breathe through the diaphragm"[15] is the often repeated advice to singers. For the untrained musician, a more helpful focus is on the muscles of the abdomen. Whereas the diaphragm (the large, flat, horizontal muscle that separates the chest cavity from the abdominal cavity) is difficult to learn to manipulate and impossible to observe, movements of the abdominal muscles are easily controlled and observed. In properly controlled breathing, these muscles are extended to cause inhalation and drawn inward to accomplish exhalation. This process pumps air into the lungs and measures its release through the windpipe and past the vocal chords. To experience proper breathing, one can simply lie with one's back on the floor and breathe deeply. The force of gravity holds the body in the proper posture and eliminates the bad habit of breathing through chest movement. While lying on his or her back, the singer can note the natural rise and fall of the abdominal muscles that pump air in and out of the lungs. When standing, having good posture and breathing with the abdominal muscles are key elements in gaining proper breath control for singing, chanting, or speaking in public.

4) *The voice is projected through resonance.* A small sound gains volume and intensity as it resonates in a chamber. In the same way that the sound of an acoustic guitar string is amplified in the guitar's box, the sound made by the vocal chords is intensified through the body's oral and nasal cavities. In order for a cantor's voice to project and be heard by all in an assembly, the mouth must be open sufficiently so as to allow the sound to escape and to provide for its amplification. As a means of measuring how far to open one's mouth in singing, try the following exercise. Place your forefinger and middle finger together and hold them horizontally between your teeth. (Rotate your wrist so that your teeth are touching the sides of your fingers.) This forces your mouth open to a comfortable degree. Next, place three fingers into your mouth. This forces the mouth open to a degree that is less comfortable but that allows for better amplification and projection of your voice. Singers learn to approximate this level of openness when they perform. In addition to the open mouth, there should be an internal sense of openness in the rear of the oral cavity. Imagine the space at the back of the mouth as being filled with a large egg. This helps to raise the soft palate and open the throat. The result is a cavernous space that rounds and broadens the vocal tone. An unpleasant, edgy tone results when the soft palate is low and unarched. Another way to envision this internal openness is to effect a yawn. If you were to try to vocalize during a full yawn, you would produce a deep, swallowed tone that doesn't resonate in the mouth. But if you open your mouth and throat to roughly two-thirds the shape of a yawn, you produce an openness that allows the sound to resonate up through the throat and into the round space of the oral cavity. This is the best shape for proper resonance of vocal sound.

5) *Vowels are the vehicle of vocal sound.* A few consonants (*m*, *n*, *l*, and *r*) can sustain vocal sound. (To hum, for example, means to form the consonant "m" with one's lips while vocalizing.) Other consonants stop vocalization as they are uttered. To pronounce the sounds "t," "p," or "s," one uses the lips, teeth, and tongue while the sound made by the vocal chords is interrupted. In order for sound and phrasing to be sustained in singing, the singer concentrates on

elongating the vowel sounds within each phrase. As an exercise in sustaining phrases, sing the following lines on a pitch. Repeat by singing on successively higher and lower pitches.

"Lay, lee, law, loh, loo"
"Mellow Molly married Maury."
"Larry loved the lady but the lady loved another lad."
"Stay awake and pray away the day."

Our discussion of the forms of ritual language concludes with an important reminder. *Mistakes are natural to the language of ritual.* Let us recall from chapter 4 that excellence is not the same thing as perfectionism. Mistakes are to be expected as ritual unfolds. No amount of preparation or rehearsal will be able to eliminate all problems that might occur. Tongues will slip, microphones will fail, lights will go out, babies will cry, worship leaders will trip, offering plates will spill. The value of being well rehearsed is that, in the face of inevitable mishaps, the worship leader can respond with good humor and grace. At such times, the attitude of the assembly will mirror that of the leader. If he or she becomes embarrassed, the people will linger in embarrassment as well. If the leader takes a mistake in stride and handles it with humor, the assembly will chuckle and soon be ready to move ahead into the next ritual moment. Aidan Kavanagh gives a helpful warning: "To be consumed with worry over making a liturgical mistake is the greatest mistake of all. Reverence is a virtue, not a neurosis, and God can take care of himself."[16]

MISCELLANEOUS WORDS

The symbols of ritual speak for themselves. They should neither be ornamented with, nor obstructed by, verbosity. Yet there are fitting times and useful ways to speak as ministers lead in the rituals of worship. Some elements of worship need to be introduced, certain announcements must be made, and occasionally a leader's words can serve to smooth transitions between ritual elements or provide hospitality. The goal for worship leaders is to speak when it is necessary, to do so effectively, and to avoid filling worship with liturgical chatter. Silence in ritual is an invitation to symbolic engagement. If the symbols of ritual speak for themselves, if they draw worshipers into the realm of virtual experience, then an effective worship leader will foster silence so that the symbols can communicate. And he or she will speak when the ritual calls for it and provide spoken commentary when hospitality and order require it. To guide the use of language, let us consider several forms of miscellaneous liturgical conversation in which the few who lead speak directly to the many who gather.

Announcements

Announcements have a place in worship. It is not helpful to expect that litur-
gies should be devoid of them. If worship is to be public and contextually rel-
evant, certain things will need to be made known. Worshipers need to know
for whom they are praying, of opportunities available to them for Christian
service, about news in the faith community, and of congregational meetings
and responsibilities. How can worship leaders alert the assembly as to important information without cluttering the liturgical landscape? They can begin
to do so by focusing on two issues: placement and language. The placement of
announcements in worship may vary as to the kind of information being given.

Announcements are given as people gather. When people assemble for worship,
they come together as disparate members of the Body of Christ. They are connected as a community of faith by two things: the unity of the Holy Spirit and
the shared knowledge of and participation in the life of the congregation. In
gathering from many places to assemble in one place, people have the regular
opportunity to learn of community events and of opportunities for Christian
service. It makes sense, then, for most of the community announcements to
take place as part of the gathering rite. Prayer announcements, however, are
better saved for a more appropriate time.

Prayer concerns are announced at the time of corporate prayer. As we saw in the
last chapter, making announcements *during* the prayers is problematic. Also
questionable is the attempt to inform the assembly as it gathers about the people and circumstances for which they will eventually pray. As a means to invite
full participation in the intercessions, a helpful approach is for the minister to
give a carefully crafted statement immediately prior to leading the prayer. One
might say, for example:

> As we draw our hearts together in prayer, let us remember Robert Diaz,
> who is scheduled to undergo heart surgery this Wednesday; Mary
> Brannigan, who is recovering from a car accident; Timothy Milward,
> who is being baptized this morning; and the people of our Property
> Committee as they consider ways to expand our facility. Let us pray. . . .

The prayer that follows might then simply mention individuals by their first
names (Robert, Mary, Timothy). Or, if the list is long, the leader might speak
of "those we have already named and those we now name in our hearts."

Announcements may be made as the assembly is dismissed. As an alternative to
giving detailed information at the time of gathering, it may make sense for
some congregations to save these announcements for the time of sending. As
they are being sent forth to serve God in the world, it makes ritual sense for
people to be informed of opportunities for service and involvement in the life
of the community. Service schedule and architecture will dictate the appro-

priateness of this approach. One congregation of my acquaintance has a social hall across from the worship space. In this congregation, people are accustomed to gathering for a time of fellowship in the social hall immediately following dismissal from worship. During this time, general announcements are shared by various members of the community.

Announcements are succinct and germane. Aesthetic sensitivity is affected more, perhaps, by a leader's use of language in giving announcements than by their placement. Let the worship leader remember that the people gather to engage in an encounter with the Hidden One. The leader's role is to serve in the shadow of the cross, not to upstage it with folksy palaver, joke telling, and cajolery. This does not mean that announcements need to be glum. Certainly the mood of the speaker should be appropriate to the information being given. But the speaker should not ramble, speak clumsily, or try to be trendy. Neither should the speaker divert the purpose of the gathering by using it as a forum to discuss irrelevant matters.

Introductions and Directions

If worship forms are to be creative, engaging, and filled with energy and meaning, there will be elements that require introduction or explanation. The following guidelines may prove useful to worship leaders who wish to speak words of introduction and guidance with ritual sensitivity.

Introducing the liturgical focus of the day is the first announcement. Even if announcements are offered primarily at the service's end, setting the stage for the focus of the gathering is accommodating both to regular worshipers and to those unfamiliar with local liturgical custom. This announcement can be brief, such as, "I welcome you today as we gather to celebrate the resurrection on this second Sunday of Easter."

New patterns of worship are introduced at the beginning. A brief word to alert people as to unfamiliar patterns of response or prayer will enable worship to flow smoothly and allow the ritual forms to speak for themselves as people engage in them.

New music is introduced at the beginning. If a new song, psalm setting, or piece of service music involves congregational involvement, it will proceed more smoothly if the assembly has time to learn it. A brief rehearsal during the announcements will facilitate learning new music. The rehearsal should be done by a leader or music minister who can both sing effectively and listen carefully as the congregation responds. More difficult sections may require repetition until they are learned.

Introductions to Scripture readings are brief and contextual. Some readings require no introduction. A parable, for example, stands on its own. One does not need to explain that Jesus often used parables as a way to teach about the kingdom of God. Other texts need to be placed in context in order for them to be understood. Reading a selection from the book of Ruth might call for a brief description about who she was and where this reading occurs in her story. Reading from Paul's epistles might call for a brief description of the circumstances that gave rise to his message. Introductions to Scripture readings can be made in a sentence or two. They are not intended to be Bible studies or homilies in miniature.

Liturgical directions are used sparingly. Because elements of ritual are symbols that speak in ways that discourse cannot, the use of speech in announcing them is not always helpful. An exception is when visitors are present who do not know the local liturgical customs. An attentive worship leader will be aware of the makeup of the gathering and adjust his or her remarks accordingly. For example, if a large number of visitors are present, as is often the case when there are baptisms, the leader may need to announce the page numbers in order to guide them to participate in the hymns or the baptismal rite. If the gathering is entirely made up of regular worshipers, such directions are *not* needed.

Worship is not Sunday school. Worship is the school of the church, says Philip Pfatteicher.[17] By this he means that Christians are formed by regular participation in the rites and sacraments of worship. Through liturgical practice, people learn to pray, learn to express their belief, learn to understand God, and learn to encounter the One who is both present and hidden. The success of such schooling does not result from worship that is filled with instruction and directions. It results from participation in rituals that communicate in their own ways on many levels. The repetition and the rhythm, and the alternation of sound and silence, music and speech, movement and rest create worlds of virtual experience that give meaning to our real worlds; they teach us how to be faithful in our response to God's interaction with us. Words of explanation do not advance the power of ritual to communicate any more than words of explanation advance the power of poetry. "The meaning of a poem can be described in words," says Pfatteicher, "but it can never be reduced to words; and so it is with all forms of art, including liturgy."[18]

There are elements of education that can help to make worshipers liturgically aware. Pastors and worship leaders may wish to offer courses that explore sacramental practice, the origins of hymns and liturgical forms, and the traditional meanings associated with worship signs and symbols. Or service bulletins may include notes about the use of a certain rite or the particular forms of music used on a given Sunday. But the educational power of the experience of worship lies in its ability to shape God's people through repeated participation in patterns that bring Christians together into the presence of God and connection with God's power and promise. Worship forms faithful people not by a hailstorm of words that batter and chip away people's resistance. It forms us through the gentle washing of the recurrent tide that makes smooth the rough places of unfaithfulness.

CONCLUSION

The objective in this chapter has been to demonstrate that issues of aesthetic responsibility extend even to what might be called the incidental aspects of liturgical expression. Whether verbal or nonverbal, expressions involving gesture, movement, repetition, music, announcements, introductions, and explanations have the capacity to draw people more deeply into the experience of worship or distract them and distance them from the encounter they seek with God. For worship leaders to take the shadow of the cross as their dwelling place is to undertake the preparation of incidentals as thoroughly as the more significant elements of worship and preaching. The purpose is not merely to be invisible, but to make Christ visible.

Our purpose throughout this text has been to engage in a discussion concerning the way we use language in worship. More can be said about the way that music speaks in worship, and the use of other arts (visual art, mime, dance, architecture, etc.) in liturgical expression. If the conversation continues as the reader experiments with the suggestions contained herein, generalizes its theories to other forms of liturgical art, or simply disagrees with the ideas presented here, the goal of this humble project is accomplished.

Notes

Introduction

1. Patrick W. Collins, *More than Meets the Eye* (New York: Paulist Press, 1983), 149.
2. Simon Blackburn, *The Oxford Dictionary of Philosophy* (Oxford: Oxford University Press, 1994), 132.
3. Stanley J. Grenz, *A Primer on Postmodernism* (Grand Rapids: Wm. B. Eerdmans Publishing Co., 1996), 24–26.
4. Ibid., 26.

Chapter 1: Art for Faith's Sake

1. Susanne K. Langer, *Philosophy in a New Key: A Study in the Symbolism of Reason, Rite, and Art* (Cambridge: Harvard University Press, 1942), 81.
2. Ibid., 100–101.
3. The passage derives from the thirteenth article, part 5 of the "Apology of the Augsburg Confession," written by Philipp Melanchthon. It is found in *The Book of Concord*, ed. Theodore G. Tappert (Philadelphia: Fortress Press, 1959), 211–12. For a full discussion of the ways that Melanchthon used the phrase "to move the heart" as a way of interpreting the nature and purpose of Christian ritual, see also Michael Aune, *"To Move the Heart": Rhetorical and Ritual in the Theology of Philip Melanchthon* (San Francisco: Christian University Press, 1994).
4. Charles L. Bartow, *Effective Speech Communication in Leading Worship* (Nashville: Abingdon Press, 1988), 15.
5. Charles L. Bartow, *God's Human Speech: A Practical Theology of Proclamation* (Grand Rapids: Wm. B. Eerdmans, 1997), 75.
6. Frank Burch Brown, *Religious Aesthetics: A Theological Study of Making and Meaning* (Princeton, N.J.: Princeton University Press, 1989), 103.
7. Susanne K. Langer, *Feeling and Form* (New York: Charles Scribner's Sons, 1953), 27.
8. Ibid., 39. By the phrase, "the logical rightness and necessity of expression," Langer refers to the artist's technique of carefully and skillfully considering the available elemental forms of a particular medium. From among them, the artist selects the proper forms and arranges them in such a way as to present the most apt rendering of the artist's aesthetic idea. This process of selection will be explored as it relates to preaching in chapter 5.
9. Brown, *Religious Aesthetics*, 86.
10. John Dewey, *Art as Experience* (New York: Minton, Balch & Co., 1943), 74.
11. D. Ndofunsu, "The Role of Prayer in the Kimbanguist Church," 590 as quoted

in Andrew Wilson-Dickson, *The Story of Christian Music: From Gregorian Chant to Black Gospel, an Illustrated Guide to All the Major Traditions of Music in Worship* (Minneapolis: Fortress Press, 1996), 180.

12. A review of the history of philosophy reveals many significant writers who have considered the nature and meaning of art and its relation to human feeling. Plato considered art to be a product of imagination that addresses itself to the emotional elements in human beings. Aristotle was most concerned with the arts of poetry and found in them the imitation of real things that are given with emotional import. Thomas Aquinas considered the nature of beauty in art and concluded that its import had to do with more than intellectual cognition. Kant saw art as the representation of real objects and recognized that in its perception, an observer could render judgments as to its beauty or ugliness, depending on how it affected the senses. Hegel viewed art as the "sensuous semblance of the Ideal" and developed a theory that categorized periods of art. Schopenhauer was interested in aesthetic contemplation as a means of escape from human slavery to the Will and identified in poetry the expression of human action, thought, and emotion. Nietzsche reflected on the aesthetics of Kant and Schopenhauer and concluded, contrary to Schopenhauer, that contemplation of beauty in art does not calm the Will, but brings it happiness and arouses its interest in sensuous things. John Dewey viewed art as the expression of human experience. This brief accounting represents the merest sampling of the numerous philosophers who have dealt with the meaning of art. To pursue further information, one can look to the books by Langer and Dewey already cited or see Frederick Copleston, S.J., *A History of Philosophy*, 10 vols. (Westminster, England: The Newman Press, 1948); Simon Blackburn, *The Oxford Dictionary of Philosophy* (Oxford: Oxford University Press, 1994); and Joseph Margolis, ed., *Philosophy Looks at the Arts* (Philadelphia: Temple University Press, 1987).

13. Langer, *Feeling and Form*, 40.

14. Hans Küng, *Art and the Question of Meaning*, trans. Edward Quinn (New York: Crossroad Publishing Co., 1981), 54.

15. Langer, *Feeling and Form*, 28.

16. The concept of the observer perceiving something new in art, though borrowed by Langer in *Feeling and Form*, 19, comes originally from Otto Baensch, "Kunst und Gefühl," printed in *Logos*, in 1923.

17. Janet R. Walton, *Art and Worship: A Vital Connection* (Collegeville, Minn.: Liturgical Press, 1991), 75.

18. As quoted in Küng, *Art and the Question of Meaning*, 52.

19. As quoted in Walton, *Art and Worship*, 76–77.

20. Walter J. Ong, S.J., *The Presence of the Word* (Minneapolis: University of Minnesota Press, 1981), 117–28.

21. Geoffrey Wainwright, *Doxology* (New York: Oxford University Press, 1980), 194–95.

22. Ibid., 117.

23. The theory of art developed by Susanne K. Langer is given in two books, already cited: *Philosophy in a New Key: A Study in the Symbolism of Reason, Rite, and Art* and its sequel, *Feeling and Form*. What Langer arrived at in the first book regarding the meaning and function of music, she developed in the second book as a full and generalized theory of art.

24. Some rhetoricians argue that there are more than two functions of language. Language has, for example, the power to name things and events. When seen

through the lens of Langer's aesthetic theory, it may be countered, this function of language might fall under either of the two functions that Langer identifies. When language functions to name a person, place, thing, or event, that naming can have a discursive quality as it allows for a symbol to stand for that about which information is conveyed. For example, "Oliver, the cat, is black," or "Advent, Christmas, and Epiphany are successive seasons in the church year." Or naming may have a nondiscursive quality when that which is named brings to mind associations, memories, emotional attachments, and attitudes that relate to that which is named. To say "Our Father," for example, is to speak a name that is associated with innumerable thoughts, feelings, and experiences. They may have to do with prayer, a person's life of faith, one's experience with father figures, feelings of support, loss, gratitude, or grief. Because memories of human experience attach themselves to names and cannot be separated from them, naming has a presentational quality and cannot avoid stimulating attitudes and feelings in people who hear the names spoken.

25. Langer, *Feeling and Form*, 209.
26. Ibid., 211.
27. Ibid., 45.
28. Ibid.
29. Ibid.
30. Ibid., 211.
31. Ibid., 228.
32. Walton, *Art and Worship*, 77.
33. Patrick W. Collins, *More than Meets the Eye* (New York: Paulist Press, 1983), 119–20.
34. Ibid., 100.
35. Ibid., 119–20.
36. Ong, *The Presence of the Word*, 311.
37. In addition to the three directions of liturgical communication that take place within the confines of worship settings, Paul Hoon recognizes that liturgy also communicates in two cultural dimensions: it speaks to and is informed by those outside the liturgical assembly. See *The Integrity of Worship: Ecumenical and Pastoral Studies in Liturgical Theology* (Nashville: Abingdon Press, 1971), 215–25.
38. Brown, *Religious Aesthetics*, 40.
39. Ibid., 86.
40. Ibid., 42.
41. Christopher L. C. E. Witcombe, "Art and Artists: Art for Art's Sake: Second Part of Five-Part Essay on Modernism," 1, Department of Art History, Sweet Briar College, available on the World Wide Web at www.arthistory.sbc.edu/artartists/modartsake.html.
42. Ibid., 4.
43. Aidan Kavanagh, *Elements of Rite* (New York: Pueblo, 1982), 54–55.
44. Jerry Evenrud, former Director for Music, Worship, and the Arts in the Evangelical Lutheran Church in America, describes himself as "a freelance advocate for music and art in worship." His lectures on the use of art and music in worship are given under the title, "Art for Faith's Sake."

Chapter 2: By Faith and Not by Sight

1. Heinrich Dornkamm, *Luther's World of Thought*, trans. Martin H. Bertram (St. Louis: Concordia Publishing House, 1958), 189. Quoted in Frank Burch

Brown, *Religious Aesthetics: A Study of Theological Making and Meaning* (Princeton, N.J.: Princeton University Press, 1989), 128–29.

2. This insight was delivered by Benjamin Cannon in a catechetical discussion among his peers.
3. As quoted in Geoffrey Wainwright, *Doxology: A Systematic Theology* (New York: Oxford University Press, 1980), 82.
4. As quoted in Ibid.
5. Ibid., 83.
6. The specific ways that God is disclosed in the sacraments of the Roman Catholic Church have been identified by David N. Power. He reports of the disclosure of the Holy Spirit given in the sacrament of baptism, the Risen Lord's strength and promise given in the anointing of the sick, the Lord's forgiveness given in penance, the uniting bond of Christ's love given in marriage, and the presence of Christ the servant given in ordination. See Power's *Unsearchable Riches: The Symbolic Nature of Liturgy* (New York: Pueblo Publishing Co., 1984), 146.
7. See Walter Brueggemann, "The Presence of God," in *The Interpreter's Dictionary of the Bible*, Supplementary Volume (Nashville: Abingdon Press, 1976), 680–83.
8. *The Mishnah*, trans. Herbert Danby (London: Oxford University Press, 1933), 450. Quoted in John E. Burkhart, *Worship: A Searching Examination of the Liturgical Experience* (Philadelphia: Westminster Press, 1982), 38.
9. Burkhart, *Worship*, 52.
10. For a historical analysis and critique of "entertainment evangelism," see Frank Senn, "'Worship Alive': An Analysis and Critique of 'Alternative Worship Services,'" in *Worship*, vol. 69, no. 3 (May, 1995), 194–224; and Frank Senn, *Christian Liturgy* (Minneapolis: Fortress Press, 1997), 687–92.
11. Richard Ward, *Speaking from the Heart: Preaching with Passion* (Nashville: Abingdon Press, 1992), 77.
12 Ibid.
13. Jana Childers, *Performing the Word: Preaching as Theater* (Nashville: Abingdon Press, 1998), 99–120.
14. Ibid., 123.
15. Charles L. Bartow, *God's Human Speech: A Practical Theology of Proclamation* (Grand Rapids: Wm. B. Eerdmans Publishing Co., 1997), 3. Bartow's use of "performative" reflects that of Ronald J. Pelias, for whom performativity involves choice, calculation, and commitment. See Pelias's *Performance Studies: The Interpretation of Aesthetic Texts* (New York: St. Martin's Press, 1992), 47–63. In the third chapter, I will draw a distinction between the present use of performative (as used by Bartow) and the way it is used by J. L. Austin.
16. Bartow, *God's Human Speech*, 3.
17. For a discussion of the ways that Christians perform the Scriptures in congregational life and action, see Richard Lischer, "Martin Luther King, Jr.: 'Performing' the Scriptures," *Anglican Theological Review*, vol. 77, no. 2 (Spring 1995), 160–72.
18. Richard Lischer, *A Theology of Preaching: The Dynamics of the Gospel* (Durham, N.C.: Labyrinth Press, 1992), 91.
19. Childers, *Performing the Word*, 123.
20. Bartow, *God's Human Speech*, 3.
21. Although the discussion here revolves around the historical figure of Jesus, he

is operating in these biblical stories as with the wisdom and power of the Χριστός or "anointed one" whom the Peter of the Synoptic Gospels recognized.

22. Henry Alford, "We Walk by Faith and Not by Sight," in *With One Voice: A Lutheran Resource for Worship* (Minneapolis: Augsburg Fortress, 1995), hymn 675.

23. See note 7. Also, for a discussion of the ways that Martin Luther dealt with God's hidden nature, see David C. Steinmetz, *Luther in Context* (Grand Rapids: Baker Books, 1995), 22–31.

24. Power, *Unsearchable Riches*, 72.

25. Philosophers and linguists disagree as to the meaning of *sign* and *symbol*. Sign, as used here and throughout this thesis, refers to that which indicates the existence, whether past, present, or future of an object, person, event, or condition. Symbols are vehicles for the conception of their objects. Susanne Langer put it succinctly: "The sign is something to act upon, or a means to command action; the symbol is an instrument of thought." See Langer's *Philosophy in a New Key: A Study in the Symbolism of Reason, Rite, and Art* (Cambridge, Mass.: Harvard University Press, 1942), 63.

26. Gordon W. Lathrop, *Holy Things: A Liturgical Theology* (Minneapolis: Fortress Press, 1993), 18.

27. Gardner C. Taylor, "A Creed for Christians," in the Odyssey Television Network's series *Great Preachers*. This sermon was delivered at Galilee Baptist Church in Trenton, N.J.

28. I am indebted to Charles L. Bartow for this insight.

29. Childers, *Performing the Word*, 109.

30. Peter E. Fink, "Perceiving the Presence of Christ," *Worship*, 58, no. 1 (January 1984): 24.

31. I. Sonne, "Synagogue," *Interpreter's Dictionary of the Bible* (Nashville: Abingdon Press, 1976), 490.

32. Justin, "The Defense and Explanation of Christian Faith and Practice," in *The Early Church Fathers*, ed. and trans. by Henry Bettenson (Oxford: Oxford University Press, 1956), 62.

33. Geoffrey Wainwright, "Preaching as Worship," in *Theories of Preaching*, ed. Richard Lischer (Durham, N.C.: Labyrinth Press, 1987), 358.

34. Bartow, *God's Human Speech*, 43.

35. Ibid.

36. Karl Barth would state the argument slightly differently. He says that it *is* God who is speaking in the sermon, but that the actual voice of the preacher is announcing what God has to say. See Barth's *Homiletics* (Louisville, Ky.: Westminster/John Knox Press, 1991), 46.

37. Lischer, *A Theology of Preaching*, 74.

38. Dietrich Bonhoeffer, "The Proclaimed Word," in Lischer, ed., *Theories of Preaching*, 28.

39. Bartow, *God's Human Speech*, 3.

40. Aidan Kavanagh, *Elements of Rite: A Handbook of Liturgical Style* (New York: Pueblo Publishing Co., 1982), 103–104.

Chapter 3: Only Say the Word

1. Walter J. Ong, S.J., *The Presence of the Word* (Minneapolis: University of Minnesota Press, 1981), 309.

2. Brian Wren, *What Language Shall I Borrow? God-Talk in Worship: A Male Response to Feminist Theology* (New York: Crossroad, 1991), 75–79.

3. S. I. Hiyakawa, *Language and Thought in Action* (New York: Harcourt Brace Jovanovich, 1972), vii, as quoted in Brian Wren, *What Language Shall I Borrow?* 75.

4. H. H. Farmer, "The I-Thou Encounter," in *Theories of Preaching*, ed. Richard Lischer (Durham, N.C.: Labyrinth Press, 1987), 125.

5. Richard Lischer, *A Theology of Preaching: The Dynamics of the Gospel* (Durham, N.C.: Labyrinth Press, 1992), 88.

6. J. L. Austin, *How to Do Things with Words* (Cambridge, Mass.: Harvard University Press, 1975), 6, see footnote 3.

7. Ronald J. Pelias, *Performance Studies: The Interpretation of Aesthetic Texts* (New York: St. Martin's Press, 1992), 15–16 and 141–50.

8. Austin, *How to Do Things with Words*, 5.

9. Ibid., 14.

10. Ibid., 32.

11. Ibid., 145–47.

12. In examining how people accomplish things with words, Austin especially addresses the issues surrounding circumstances that render performatory or illocutionary utterances inoperative. He chases down six categories of circumstance that make for infelicitous performance and captures them under two classifications: misfires and abuses. The kinds of statements that make for performatory misfires include what Austin calls misinvocations, misexecutions, misapplications, flaws, and hitches. Under the classification of abuses he includes statements that are uttered as insincerities. See pp. 17–18. Austin's purpose in this program is not only to identify the performatory force of language but to demonstrate the ways that this force can be impeded or rendered impotent. Because our purpose is to focus on the power of language, we will draw from Austin's study only those elements that demonstrate the force of felicitous performance. From these, we can abstract the concept of divine power at work in human liturgical expression.

13. Ibid., 48.

14. Ibid.

15. The notion of God speaking is, naturally, a metaphor that plays on the anthropomorphic sense that God uses the human capacity of locution. But it is a strong metaphor that runs throughout Scripture and aids in our understanding of who God is and how God chooses to relate to people.

16. In early Jewish cultic use, "hallelujah" did function in the imperative mood; with "hallel" being the command to "praise" and "jah" (or "yah") indicating that "Yahweh" is the object. In later and modern usage, "hallelujah" functions as an interjection and not a verb. See M. Newman, "Hallelujah" in *The Interpreter's Dictionary of the Bible*, vol. 2 (Nashville: Abingdon Press, 1962), 514–15.

17. *The United Methodist Hymnal: Book of United Methodist Worship* (Nashville: United Methodist Publishing House, 1989), 20.

18. Ibid., 39.

19. See note 4, chap. 2, which refers to the assertion that God is present in worship in special and varying degrees.

20. This statement of absolution is a close paraphrase of that found in *Lutheran Book of Worship* (Minneapolis: Augsburg Publishing House, 1978), 56. It has been modified here to render the statement in more inclusive language.

21. *Baptism, Eucharist, and Ministry, Faith and Order Paper 111* (Geneva: World Council of Churches, 1982), 2.

22. Ibid., 13.

23. James M. Kittleson, *Luther the Reformer: The Story of the Man and His Career* (Minneapolis: Augsburg Publishing House, 1986), 54.

24. *Luther's Works*, vol. 54, ed. Helmut T. Lehman (Philadelphia: Fortress Press, 1958), 89.

25. Richard Lischer, "Preaching and the Rhetoric of Promise," in *Word and World*, vol. 8, no. 1 (Winter 1988): 71.

26. Ibid.

27. Ibid.

28. Karl Barth, *Homiletics*, trans. Geoffrey W. Bromiley and Donald E. Daniels (Louisville, Ky.: Westminster/John Knox Press, 1991), 45.

29. Ibid., 47.

30. Ibid., 49.

31. Ibid., 71–74.

32. Richard Lischer alludes to the performatory power of preaching by drawing his reader's attention to the work of J. R. Searle, who uses the category of promise as a test case in his analysis of illocutionary language. See Richard Lischer, "Preaching and the Rhetoric of Promise," 71, note 14.

33. Barbara Brown Taylor, "Dare to Preach," in *Concise Encyclopedia of Preaching*, ed. Richard Lischer and William Willimon (Louisville, Ky.: Westminster John Knox Press, 1995), 512.

34. Ibid.

35. Ibid.

Chapter 4: The Hiddenness of Excellence

1. Beth Luey, *Handbook for Academic Authors* (Cambridge: Cambridge University Press, 1997), 11.

2. Karl Barth, *Homiletics*, trans. Geoffrey W. Bromily and Donald E. Daniels (Louisville, Ky.: Westminster/ John Knox Press, 1991), 72.

3. Ibid., 73.

4. Dietrich Bonhoeffer, *The Cost of Discipleship*, trans. R. H. Fuller and Irmgard Booth (New York: Touchstone Books; Simon and Schuster, 1995), 157.

5. Ibid.

6. Ibid., 158.

7. Ibid.

8. Ibid., 159.

9. The temptation to lean on one's greatness in the pulpit was evident early in the life of the church. In the fourth century, St. John Chrysostom dealt with the problem of the great but slothful preacher: "For though the preacher may have great ability (and this one would only find in a few), not even in this case is he released from perpetual toil. For since preaching does not come by nature, but by study, suppose a man to reach a high standard of it, this will then forsake him if he does not cultivate his power by constant application and exercise. So that there is greater labor for the wiser than for the unlearned." John Chrysostom, "The Temptations of Greatness," in *Theories of Preaching*, ed. Richard Lischer (Durham, N.C.: The Labyrinth Press, 1987), 44.

10. Charles L. Bartow, *God's Human Speech: A Practical Theology of Proclamation* (Grand Rapids: Wm. B. Eerdmans Publishing Co., 1997), 74.

11. Barth, *Homiletics*, 90.

12. C. H. Dodd, *The Apostolic Preaching and Its Developments* (London: Hodder and Stoughton, 1937), 13.

13. For a discussion of how the preacher can exegete the congregational context as an important step in sermon preparation, see Leonora Tubbs Tisdale, *Preaching as Local Theology and Folk Art* (Minneapolis: Fortress Press, 1997).
14. Exceptions to this norm might be the intentional reading of a sermon by a prominent historical figure, such as Luther or Wesley, or the local reading of a special pastoral address from a district president or synodical bishop.
15. The phrase "real enough to enter" comes from Charles L. Bartow, *The Preaching Moment* (Nashville: Abingdon Press, 1980), 14. Bartow is not only the source of this insight, but also the preacher under discussion.
16. Barth, *Homiletics*, 89–90.
17. James E. Miller, *A Little Book for Preachers: 101 Ideas for Better Sermons* (Minneapolis: Augsburg Publishing House, 1996), 23.
18. The poem "Prophets of a Future Not Our Own" is attributed to martyred archbishop of Nicaragua, Oscar Romero.

Chapter 5: Treasure in Earthen Vessels

1. David Buttrick disagrees. "While preaching is not an art, it is artful," he says. He then proceeds to demonstrate the artful characteristics of good preaching. It may be "compelling and exquisitely formed," crafted by preachers who have learned the skills of the trade. See *Homiletic* (Philadelphia: Fortress Press, 1987), 37.
2. Louise M. Rosenblatt, *The Reader, the Text, the Poem* (Carbondale, Ill.: Southern Illinois University Press, 1978), 12.
3. Gail Ramshaw, *Liturgical Language: Keeping It Metaphoric, Making It Inclusive* (Collegeville, Minn.: Liturgical Press, 1996), 10.
4. See Mark Steven Gelter, "'Toy Story' — Infinitely Far Beyond 'Tron'," *Unlimited Vision On-Line*, 1996. In this Web review, Gelter compares Disney's first computer-generated film attempt with *Toy Story*: "Remember *Tron*? In 1984, Disney looked to make history with the first movie to feature computer-generated graphics. Movie crashed. Well, movie was dumb, actors were dumb, computer graphics made everybody look like they had been dipped in neon paint. But computer effects didn't die. Today they are so prevalent that often you don't even realize they're being used. And while it's obvious that films like *Jurassic Park* and *Terminator 2* wouldn't even exist without the technology, the idea of a 100% C.G. feature film still dredges up bad *Tron* vibes. Well, not to worry, tech fans. *Toy Story* not only wipes away those vibes, it's just a darn good movie, pixilated or not."
5. Fred B. Craddock, *As One without Authority* (Nashville: Abingdon Press, 1985), 80.
6. Susanne K. Langer, *Philosophy in a New Key* (Cambridge, Mass.: Harvard University Press, 1942), 260.
7. Ibid., 234.
8. Fred B. Craddock, *Preaching* (Nashville: Abingdon Press, 1985), 122.
9. Richard A. Jensen, "The Story Is the Point," in *Academy Accents*, vol. 8, no. 4, (Winter 1993): 4.
10. Christine M. Smith, *Weaving the Sermon: Preaching in a Feminist Perspective* (Louisville, Ky.: Westminster/John Knox Press, 1989), 11–12.
11. Ibid., 13.
12. Reynolds Price, *Learning a Trade: A Craftsman's Notebooks: 1955–1997* (Durham, N.C.: Duke University Press, 1998), viii.

13. Ibid.
14. Peter Elbow, *Writing with Power: Techniques for Mastering the Writing Process* (New York: Oxford University Press, 1998), 79.
15. Ibid.
16. Jana Childers, *Performing the Word: Preaching as Theater* (Nashville: Abingdon Press, 1998), 15–35.
17. John M. Mulder, "Call," in *Concise Encyclopedia of Preaching*, ed. Richard Lischer and William Willimon (Louisville, Ky.: Westminster John Knox Press, 1995), 59.
18. Ibid.
19. Karl Barth, *Homiletics* (Louisville, Ky.: Westminster/John Knox Press, 1991), 68.
20. Ruth Duck's eight-step process involves: 1) beginning with prayer, 2) engaging the imagination, 3) brainstorming, 4) focusing, 5) letting the words flow, 6) taking a break, 7) revising, and 8) learning from feedback. See *Finding Words for Worship* (Louisville, Ky.: Westminster John Knox Press, 1995), 54–58.
21. Childers, *Performing the Word*, 19.
22. See, for example, Ramshaw, *Liturgical Language*; Richard Lischer, *The Preacher King: Martin Luther King, Jr., and the Word That Moved America* (New York: Oxford University Press, 1995), where he explores the tropes that were used by King in sermons and speeches; and Buttrick, *Homiletic*, in which he addresses the use of metaphor in preaching.
23. This National Public Radio interview was broadcast by WUNC, Chapel Hill, N.C., on November 15, 1998.
24. Kim Addonizio and Dorianne Laux, *The Poet's Companion: A Guide to the Pleasures of Writing Poetry* (New York: W. W. Norton & Co., 1997), 86.
25. James J. Kilpatrick, *The Writer's Art* (Kansas City: Andrews and McMeel, 1984), 43.
26. Ibid.
27. Susanne K. Langer, *Feeling and Form* (New York: Charles Scribner's Sons, 1953), 39.
28. Mark Twain, as quoted in Kilpatrick, *The Writer's Art*, 28.
29. Ibid.
30. Mark Twain, as quoted in Garry Wills, *Lincoln at Gettysburg: Words That Remade America* (New York: Simon and Schuster, 1992), 164.
31. Addonizio and Laux, *The Poet's Companion*, 86.
32. Kilpatrick, *The Writer's Art*, 118.
33. For example, Jana Childers, in *Performing the Word*, offers a set of exercises that allows the reader to practice powers of observation.
34. All of the examples in the exercises in chapters 5 and 6 are original unless otherwise credited in the text.
35. Barbara Brown Taylor, "One Step at a Time," in *The Preaching Life* (Cambridge, Mass.: Cowley Publications, 1993), 93.
36. Kilpatrick, *The Writer's Art*, 1.
37. Taylor, *The Preaching Life*, 40.
38. Jane Smiley, *Moo* (New York: Ivy Books, 1995), 226.
39. Arthur Quinn, *Figures of Speech: 60 Ways to Turn a Phrase* (Salt Lake City: Gibbs M. Smith, 1985), 29, 98.
40. Ibid., 21.
41. Ibid., 2.
42. Ibid., 5.

43. Ibid., 6.
44. As quoted by Quinn, *Figures of Speech*, 12.
45. Kilpatrick, *The Writer's Art*, 105.
46. Gertrude Stein, as quoted by Addonizio and Laux, *The Poet's Companion*, 152.
47. Kilpatrick, *The Writer's Art*, 101.
48. Winston Churchill, as quoted by Kilpatrick, *The Writer's Art*, 101.
49. As quoted by Paul Scott Wilson, *A Concise History of Preaching* (Nashville: Abingdon Press, 1992), 112.
50. Quinn, *Figures of Speech*, 67.
51. Kilpatrick, *The Writer's Art*, 105.
52. Charles Bartow has made theological hay out of this quality of the metonym. He has shown, according to Reformed tradition, that the breaking of the bread and the pouring of the cup in Communion are metonymic figures that represent the presence of Christ in the world. Likewise, the reading of the Scriptures in worship serves metonymically to direct us to the presence of Christ in worship. See *God's Human Speech* (Grand Rapids: Wm. B. Eerdmans Publishing Co., 1997), 16–20.
53. Addonizio and Laux, *The Poet's Companion*, 94.
54. Kilpatrick, *The Writer's Art*, 97.
55. Ibid., 98.
56. Addonizio and Laux, *The Poet's Companion*, 95.
57. Price, *Learning a Trade*, 9.
58. Elbow, *Writing with Power*, 79.
59. Kilpatrick, *The Writer's Art*, 99.
60. Ibid., 101.
61. Ibid.
62. Buttrick, *Homiletic*, 121.
63. Ibid., 123.
64. Kilpatrick, *The Writer's Art*, 97–105.
65. Austin Lovelace, *Anatomy of a Hymn* (Chicago: GIA Publications, Inc., 1965), 93–94.
66. Lischer, *The Preacher King*, 120.
67. Kilpatrick, *The Writer's Art*, 102.
68. Reynolds Price, "Jesus," from *The Collected Poems* (New York: Scribner, 1997), 180.
69. Kilpatrick, *The Writer's Art*, 103.
70. Ibid.
71. Addonizio and Laux, *The Poet's Companion*, 141.
72. Kilpatrick, *The Writer's Art*, 108.
73. Wills, *Lincoln at Gettysburg*, 149.
74. Addonizio and Laux, *The Poet's Companion*, 186.
75. Clyde Fant, "Memory," in Lischer and Willimon, *Concise Encyclopedia of Preaching*, 331.

Chapter 6: The Need as Deep as Life

1. Kathleen Hughes, *Lay Presiding: The Art of Leading Prayer, American Essays in Liturgy* (Collegeville, Minn.: Liturgical Press, 1988), 16.
2. C. S. Lewis, "Modern Translations of the Bible," as quoted in Louis Weil, *Gathered to Pray: Understanding Liturgical Prayer* (Cambridge, Mass.: Cowley Publications, 1986), 92.

3. Hughes, *Lay Presiding*, 24.
4. Ibid.
5. Weil, *Gathered to Pray*, 11.
6. Ibid., 12.
7. An exception to the suggestion that the Prayers of the People be prepared locally occurs when the prayers are prepared as propers to unite congregations in prayer in special circumstances. For example, a denominationally prepared prayer might be used on a given Sunday to unite Christians in a unified expression of their tradition. Or churches of different denominations might choose to use an agreed on form of prayer to celebrate Christian unity, as on the World Day of Prayer. Yet, even on such occasions, there is room for locally prepared prayers to be spoken alongside published prayers.
8. Hughes, *Lay Presiding*, 29.
9. Dietrich Bonhoeffer, *Life Together* (London: SCM Press, 1949), 46–47.
10. Hughes, *Lay Presiding*, 39.
11. Brian Wren, *What Language Shall I Borrow?* (New York: Crossroad, 1991), 144.
12. Ibid.
13. William H. Willimon, *Preaching and Leading Worship: The Pastor's Handbook* (Louisville, Ky.: The Westminster Press, 1984), 44.
14. Ibid., 1.

Chapter 7: In the Shadow of the Cross

1. Aidan Kavanagh, *Elements of Rite: A Handbook of Liturgical Style* (New York: Pueblo Publishing Co., 1982), 103.
2. Ibid.
3. Louis Dupre, as quoted in *Liturgy*, ed. Gabe Huck and Vivian Carter (Chicago: Liturgy Training Publications, 1994), 77.
4. Don E. Saliers, "Christian Liturgy as Eschatological Art," in *Arts: The Arts in Religion and Theological Studies*, vol. 1 (1999), 16–17.
5. Kavanagh, *Elements of Rite*, 101.
6. Ibid.
7. Evelyn Underhill, *Worship* (New York: Harper and Row Publishers, 1936), as quoted in *Liturgy*, 65.
8. Kavanagh, *Elements of Rite*, 53.
9. For a discussion of the place of hospitality in worship leadership, see Robert W. Hovda, *Strong, Loving, and Wise: Presiding in Liturgy* (Collegeville, Minn.: Liturgical Press, 1976), 48–49.
10. Jana Childers, *Performing the Word: Preaching as Theater* (Nashville: Abingdon Press, 1998), 137.
11. Janet Schlichting, "What Is Procession?" in *Liturgy*, 69–70.
12. J. D. Crichton, *The Once and Future Liturgy* (Dublin: Veritas Publications, 1977), 92.
13. Kavanagh, *Elements of Rite*, 52.
14. John Bell and Graham Maule, "Ten Golden Rules for Enabling the Least Confident of People to Teach New Songs to the Most Cynical of Congregations," in *Heaven Shall Not Wait: Wild Goose Songs, Volume One: Songs of Creation, the Incarnation, and the Life of Jesus* (Chicago: GIA Publications), 124.
15. To breathe through the diaphragm means to use this muscle in acquiring a full breath and in exhaling the breath in measured flow. The diaphragm is moved involuntarily, however, by voluntary movement of the abdominal

muscles. While it is correct to say that good breath support involves breathing "through the diaphragm," it is the abdominal muscles that initiate diaphragmatic movement.

16. Kavanagh, *Elements of Rite*, 31.
17. See Philip H. Pfatteicher, *The School of the Church: Worship and Christian Formation* (Valley Forge, Pa.: Trinity Press International, 1995).
18. Ibid.. 71.

Scripture Index

Author Index

Printed in the United States
67490LVS00003B/190-249